Love Laughter and Longevity

I0112249

GLOBAL
PUBLISHING
GROUP

Global Publishing Group
Australia • New Zealand • Singapore • America • London

Love Laughter and Longevity

The Art and Science of Wellbeing

Janni Goss

First Edition 2017

Copyright © 2017 Janni Goss

All rights are reserved. The material contained within this book is protected by copyright law, no part may be copied, reproduced, presented, stored, communicated or transmitted in any form by any means without prior written permission.

National Library of Australia
Cataloguing-in-Publication entry:

Creator: Goss, Janni, author.

Title: Love laughter and longevity : the art and science of wellbeing /
Janni Goss.

1st ed.
ISBN: 9781922118813 (paperback)

Subjects: Well-being.
Health.
Laughter--Psychological aspects.
Love--Psychological aspects.
Longevity.

Published by Global Publishing Group
PO Box 517 Mt Evelyn, Victoria 3796 Australia
Email Info@GlobalPublishingGroup.com.au

Printed in China

For further information about orders:
Phone: +61 3 9739 4686 or Fax +61 3 8648 6871

Dear Reader, this book is dedicated to you…

Janni Goss

Acknowledgements

Over many years I have been taught and inspired by many people, and encouraged, supported and provided with opportunities by them. During my career as a physiotherapy clinician and educator, I have learnt much from my colleagues, students, patients, clients and carers, and sincerely thank them.

On my own journey to wellbeing, I have learnt many methods and techniques to develop self-awareness and outsmart stress. I would like to express my appreciation to Dr Frank Wildman and his colleagues, Dr Martin Seligman, Steve Wells, Dr Ian Gawler, Dr Patch Adams, Richmond Heath and Dr David Berceli. Many other practitioners and authors have enhanced my learning via their books, articles and webinars on a multitude of topics on health and wellbeing.

I am extremely grateful to Dr Madan Kataria and his wife Madhuri of Laughter Yoga International who introduced me to Laughter Yoga in November 2000, which has had a profound influence on my life. Special thanks to my LaughWA colleagues, as well as Merv Neal and Sebastien Gendry. Kimmy O'Meara has been an inspiration in her successful quest to introduce Laughter Yoga to Rwanda. Her amazing laughter always triggers mine!

I have received much positive support in diverse ways over many years from Barbara Leonard, Glenys Davies, Anne Beuchat, Sister Bernadette Ziesing, Eva Bett and Yanni Georgiou. Dorothy James has recently come into my life and assisted me in achieving my goals. My heartfelt thanks to you all and others too numerous to mention!

I would like to acknowledge the influence of my loving and nurturing parents, Keith and Keyse Bolleman, who always supported me to

achieve my dreams. I learnt a great deal about parenting from them, and even more from my son, Simon. May you, Miyo and Ethan have a long, loving and healthy life together.

This book has resulted from a strong desire to share what I have learnt and taught about outsmarting stress, and optimising health and wellbeing. It has only come about thanks to the support and encouragement of Darren Stephens and his team at Global Publishing, to whom I owe a huge debt of gratitude. Thank you for your commitment, guidance and patience.

Finally, this book would never have been completed without the exceptional computer skills and support of Diana Roosevelt, my P.A. (Personal Angel).

Contents

FREE BONUS GIFT

Thank you for investing in my book and in your own health and wellbeing.

To express my appreciation,
I would like to offer you the opportunity
to download the following from my website:
- The Laughter Prescription
- The Benefits of Laughter
- Simple Pleasures

Please visit www.JanniGoss.com to claim these resources.

We Who Laugh … Last!

Foreword

I am delighted to have been invited to introduce you to this book. Not only does Janni Goss explain and illustrate the benefits of laughter, she also provides wide-ranging information about how to achieve health and wellbeing and enjoy your longevity. Janni was personally trained by me in November 2000 and has had considerable influence on the development of Laughter Yoga in Western Australia.

For a long time I have been dedicated to promoting the healing properties of laughter, and as a physician, I was well aware of the negative consequences of stress on health. When I started the Laughter Yoga movement in 1995 with my wife, Madhuri, I had no idea that it would become a social movement throughout 106 countries, contributing to health and wellbeing.

It is very evident in our modern world that stress is a major cause of chronic disease, depression and for some, dementia. Understanding the causes and consequences of stress and having many strategies to deal with it are integral to the success of our relationships at home and at work. Lifestyle factors play a big part in influencing our health and wellbeing.

In this book, Janni explores many aspects of the effects of stress and shares her experiences of finding numerous ways to deal with it, choosing a healthier lifestyle and contributing to healthy longevity. As a Laughter Yoga teacher and ambassador, Janni has added these skills to her knowledge and experience as a physiotherapist. She is a passionate

advocate for including Laughter Yoga in chronic disease management, rehabilitation and aged care, as well as in education and the corporate and business world. Health professionals and family carers can also benefit from the information in this book. In fact, anyone who wishes to outsmart stress and make the most of life will be inspired by this book.

By inviting laughter and many other positive strategies into your life, I hope that you will achieve good health, peace and joy and share this wellbeing with the people in your life.

Dr. Madan Kataria
Founder of Laughter Yoga Movement

Introduction

Dear Reader! You may very well ask, why am I writing this book? Why has health and wellbeing become a topic of great interest to me? I have had an interesting life with numerous and varied challenges over many years. I became very interested in finding out about stress, what causes my stress, how I react and respond to it and searching for many ways to outsmart it.

I came to the conclusion that I need to take responsibility for my own health and wellbeing – we all need to do so!

To be successful, we need to have adequate 'health literacy', so over many decades I have learnt a great deal about the structure and function of the human body and how vulnerable it can be. We need to have healthy lifestyles, make the right choices and particularly access multiple strategies for stress reduction. One of the most significant ways to reduce stress, boost your immune system and contribute to health and wellbeing is a form of laughter therapy called Laughter Yoga.

All the knowledge and experience about health and disease I have gained directly from significant teachers. I have also sought information from webinars, articles, books, etc., in fact, multiple sources.

I thought it might be helpful to you if I distilled and clarified this information to make it more accessible and user friendly. This book is a collection of information that I have utilised and which I hope will prompt you to make the right decisions to achieve a long, healthy and happy life. It is up to each of us.

So who will get the most benefit from this book? Perhaps people in their fifties and over will find this book useful. The so-called 'baby boomers' may be dealing with the needs of four generations of people! Known as the 'sandwich generation', this particular group may have adult children (some still living at home) as well as grandchildren. They may have frail, elderly parents who require more care and attention. They have all this responsibility at the same time as they are continuing to work in their career, occupation or profession. If they also have a carer role for a family member, that is an extra demand.

Many grandparents care for their grandchildren so that their parents can work full-time. Other grandparents are parenting their grandchildren full-time as the children's parents are no longer able to provide care for them. This is often due to challenging circumstances which have traumatised the children. As people get older, a spouse may have to take care of their partner who may have chronic health problems or the onset of dementia.

Some carers are known for not taking care of themselves because they feel that they have to put other people's needs ahead of their own. Some carers forego paid employment to manage their caring responsibilities. This can have a significant negative impact on their finances, as well as their health and wellbeing. Carers need all the support and respite possible so that they are able to continue in their caring role.

Even the parents of new babies need to care for themselves with new responsibilities and sleep deprivation to challenge them.

So whatever your age or roles in life, this book may assist you to understand the factors contributing to healthy longevity and guide you to taking personal responsibility.

We often have good intentions and set ourselves useful goals. Perhaps, like me, you manage for a while and then bad habits reappear! Is the human body so complex and amazing that we need to totally respect and nurture ourselves? If we realise how truly spectacular the structure and function of our body is, surely we would want to keep it in optimal condition. Maybe this requires a degree of self-awareness, self-appreciation, self-love, enlightened self-interest and at the least, self-preservation.

> "If you don't look after your body —
> you won't have anywhere to live!"

Self-compassion is not about narcissism or self-indulgence but underpins an approach to life which nurtures body, mind and spirit. The body is made up of trillions of cells, all requiring nourishment and capable of communicating with each other. From the meeting of two cells, which have divided and differentiated, we have multiple systems and organs which interact and are regulated, for the most part, automatically. For instance, we have a circulatory system, digestive and waste disposal system, and an amazing brain which regulates and coordinates and is the prime mover for our thoughts, beliefs and actions. Our nervous system also provides an alarm and a relaxation system. Just stop and think for a moment of all the activities happening in your body and mind at this very moment.

You are breathing in oxygen and exhaling carbon dioxide. Your heart is pumping oxygen-rich blood throughout your body to nourish and replenish your cells. Your liver and kidneys are processing waste products and your pancreas is producing insulin. Your digestive system is absorbing nutrients, leading to waste disposal.

Your skin literally holds you together in a protective, sensitive and flexible layer which helps to regulate your temperature and warns you about noxious stimuli. When you cut or damage it, the skin has a great capacity to heal, as does our bony skeleton which supports us against gravity and allows us to perform multiple movements by the muscles attached to it. As well as the mechanics of the body, we have sensations, feelings and emotions and the ability to learn, love and laugh.

So let us explore how we can best look after this body, mind and spirit which has been gifted to us and treat ourselves with the respect that we deserve!

> "Be careful of reading health books,
> you may die of a misprint." — Mark Twain

Chapter 1

✿

Outsmart Stress for Healthy Longevity

Chapter 1

Outsmart Stress for Healthy Longevity

> "The goal is to die young as late as possible."
> — Dr Bradford Weeks

According to the Mayo Clinic, 75-95% of our dis-ease (that is physical and psychological illness) is caused by stress. So we need to recognise what triggers our stress (known as a stressor) and how we react or respond to it. The health consequences of chronic stress are very significant.

So, what is STRESS? Stress, basically, is anything occurring in your environment which you need to respond to but don't have the personal resources to do so. We respond to many demands in our everyday life competently and this is how we achieve our goals in life, whether it is at work, within the family or in our personal life. This is known as eustress and is essential to our success in life.

However, we regularly encounter stimuli and challenges to which we need to respond – the alarm going off in the morning, getting to work on time, deadlines, work expectations, parental responsibilities and financial commitments. Every day is full of them and we also have many daily achievements stimulated by eustress (the good kind). But when we are stuck in traffic, experience work pressure, have a sick child, or all our bills arrive at once, we can feel stressed and a bit overwhelmed. How we perceive these events influences how we react to them. They are often neutral events but we can choose the meaning that we attach to them.

> *"The primary cause of unhappiness is never the situation but your thoughts about it."*
> *— Eckhart Tolle*

When the alarm goes off in the morning, how do you react? Are you shocked that your day of responsibility has begun? Or are you grateful for a good night's sleep and a day of possible achievements and pleasures?

When you are stuck in traffic, do you get frustrated and angry, heading towards road rage perhaps? Or are you grateful that maybe the accident that caused the delay doesn't involve you? Or maybe you reflect on alternative forms of transport or routes to avoid future hold-ups. Maybe you listen to music and sing along, practice your pelvic floor exercises or just focus on your breathing and relax.

Dealing with stress effectively often involves remaining calm and focussed, assessing the situation, creating solutions or accepting what you can't change. You can decide to avoid the situation in future, if possible, modify the stressor or change how you react to it. We often react habitually to challenging circumstances, rather than make a measured assessment and respond more appropriately.

This is where emotional intelligence comes in. This is the ability to recognise our own emotions and respond appropriately. It also involves recognising the emotions of other people and responding suitably. This may result in empathy, kindness and compassion as well.

We have been told, "Love thy neighbour as thyself." This implies that we need to love ourselves first, so that we can know how to love our neighbour.

If we truly love ourselves, we need to understand the causes and effects of stress in our lives. We need to be prepared to inform ourselves and learn multiple strategies to outsmart stress, to notice our own early warning signs of stress and use healthy coping strategies to defuse the stress and remain calm and focussed. Resilience is the ability to bounce back from the challenges that life throws at us. We learn from our mistakes and failures, building on our experiences as we become older and wiser.

> "Love is the ultimate coach. Do what you love, let love guide you and let love inspire you." — Robert Holden

What is the problem with unhealthy coping strategies?

When we are continually stressed, we do NOT enjoy how we are feeling! We may feel anxious, frustrated, angry, sad, depressed, powerless, isolated or pessimistic. These are negative emotions which create negative chemicals in our bodies, such as cortisol and adrenalin, because our stress response has been switched on. It has been suggested to me that we use the term 'uncomfortable emotions' which is probably a good idea and reduces their potency.

Acute stress triggers the fight or flight response, or for some people, a freeze response results. This helps to preserve us from severe threat or danger so that we can protect ourselves. In our ancestors, this response was activated by encountering sabretooth tigers and other predators. So fighting or running away was a very appropriate response!

However, with the pressures and demands of modern living, this stress response is frequently in the 'on' position. You know what it feels like; you suddenly sense a threat and you are immediately alert to take appropriate action. Your pulse and blood pressure rises, your muscles tense for action, your mouth is dry and your palms sweaty.

At the same time, cortisol and adrenalin are released into your bloodstream, your liver supplies glycogen to your muscles, and less important systems shut down. These include the digestive system and the healing and regenerative system. When your cortisol levels are continuously high from chronic stress, the immune system doesn't function as well. This, combined with a loss of healing and regeneration, compromises your health. This is why existing conditions may worsen with chronic stress and we are more susceptible to infections such as colds and flu.

With constant stress, we are in a state of 'hypervigilance' or 'hyperarousal'. When I have been in that state, I say that my brain is on 'red alert'. In fact, Dr Rick Hanson, a neuropsychologist who specialises in Positive Neuroplasticity, calls this state of high vigilance a 'red brain'. He explains that our brains are wired up to be constantly on the lookout for danger and that we have a negativity bias. This means our brain tends to gravitate toward negative thoughts.

By continually thinking about the past negative and traumatic events in our lives, we are just reinforcing these pathways. We can actually re-traumatise ourselves by remembering these events. The brain cannot differentiate between experiencing, re-telling or re-imagining these events. Thus, we experience the same negative (or uncomfortable) emotions provoked by the original experience, whether it is fear, anger or anxiety.

As we cannot change the past (only learn from it), wouldn't it be preferable to focus on the positive, meaningful, amusing, beautiful and enjoyable memories that we have accumulated?

According to Dr Hanson, we need to **'Take in the Good'**. That is, take notice of all the small but enjoyable moments each day, savour them, experience them and wire them into the positive circuits in the brain so that we develop a positivity bias. This practice also helps us, along with other strategies like meditation, to develop a 'green brain' which is calm, focussed and non-judgemental, creating a sense of peace and wellbeing, quite the opposite of the vigilant, uptight red brain with which we might be more familiar.

So the first step to outsmart stress is self-awareness, recognising your stress triggers and how you react to them. Are you aware of your early warning signs of stress?

You might like to check the following list to see if any of these symptoms are relevant to you. Remember, the more aware you are, the earlier you can intervene with a healthy choice to change how you feel, so that the situation does not progress to a sense of being overwhelmed and powerless, resulting in unhealthy coping strategies.

Some symptoms of stress:

Physical	fatigue, headache, muscle aches, sleeping and eating problems, worsening of chronic conditions and increased likelihood of illness
Emotional	guilt, anger, loneliness, depression and anxiety
Mental	forgetfulness, difficulty making decisions and poor attention

Interpersonal	withdrawal, blaming, irritability, impatience and sensitivity to criticism
Spiritual	feelings of alienation, loss of hope, purpose and meaning

My signs of stress are fatigue and irritability, expressed by being impatient, which is a clear, early-warning sign for me, I must confess. In this state, I have been known to utter four letter words in response to minor inconveniences and events!

Muscle tension is a common consequence of stress, resulting in a clenched jaw, hunched shoulders and for some, headache, neck or backache. We all share the physiology of the fight or flight response, which is triggered in the primitive part of the reptilian brain. However, our own particular responses to stress are unique and can manifest in many ways, as the list above demonstrates. I have to admit that I have experienced quite a few of the stress symptoms above, but many of them long ago.

What are coping strategies?

When we are stressed, we want to change how we feel. When experiencing physical or emotional pain, which is expressed by negative emotions, we often make choices involving chemicals to improve the situation. Comfort food is a prime example of trying to soothe ourselves and trying to reduce the distress.

Time for a confession! Many years ago my favourite comfort food was a chocolate malted thick shake! That icy cold, creamy, sweet drink was indeed pleasurable – but that pleasure was short-lived and didn't solve the causes of my stress. Comfort foods often consist of carbohydrates

which tend to add to one's circumference! Chocolate, of course, is a favourite, but the type of chocolate does matter. Large quantities of chocolate with low cocoa and high fat and sugar content are not recommended. But for high content cocoa and low sugar (which may have a slightly bitter taste) one to two squares seem to do the trick. This type of chocolate has many healthy ingredients which justify enjoying this pleasure sparingly but regularly.

Keeping an emergency chocolate supply is wise and of course makes an excellent gift for friends. So this example demonstrates the difference between unhealthy and healthy coping strategies.

Why do we drink alcohol?

Is it because we enjoy the taste and it helps us to relax at the end of the day? Does it enhance a meal and lubricate social occasions? Do we stick with the recommended 1-2 glasses per day? If not, why not? Are we so stressed and unhappy that we self-medicate with alcohol to try and diminish the pain?

We are well-informed by health professionals and the media of the negative consequences of excessive alcohol intake but do we take any notice? There is confusing data about the benefits of say, red wine, drunk in moderation. But daily intake will eventually take its toll on your brain and your liver. Alcohol free days (AFD's) are recommended to allow for their recovery. Alcohol may blur awareness of physical and emotional pain. Seeking help and sharing the problem in order to create effective solutions is a healthy coping strategy. Notice your early warning signs of stress and be proactive.

Other chemicals such as caffeine, nicotine, over-the-counter and prescription drugs may also be over-used to try to mitigate the effects of

stress. They will eventually have long-term consequences. Accidental overdose with opioids is on the increase. Illegal drugs seem to be readily available to those who crave them. All these chemicals have toxic side effects which contribute to disease, adding to the negative effects of stress and compounding the situation. Therefore, the combination of a chronic stress response and unhealthy coping strategies can contribute to obesity, high blood pressure, cardiovascular disease, stroke, diabetes, depression and for some, dementia.

This continuum of chronic diseases may be first recognised as metabolic syndrome, which is characterised by weight gain, raised cholesterol, high blood pressure, inactivity and unhealthy lifestyle choices including smoking and drinking alcohol.

This all contributes to the ageing process!

This situation can be reversed by determined commitment to healthy lifestyle choices around nutrition, hydration, breathing, sleep, physical activity and socialisation and emotional wellbeing. Our healthy longevity depends on it.

So take a look again at your own life.

- What triggers your stress?

  _____

  _____

- How do you react?

  _____

  _____

- What are your early warning signs?

  _____

  _____

- What strategies do you use to reduce your stress?

  _____

  _____

- Are they healthy or unhealthy?

  _____

  _____

- Do you resort to using 'chemicals'? If so, what are they?

  _____

  _____

- What negative emotions do you experience?

  _____

  _____

- Do you really understand the stress response and how it affects you?

  _____

  _____

Let me share some healthy strategies to use when you are feeling uptight.

Breathing

Yes, taking several mindful, slow, deep breaths can help to calm you and your nervous system. This allows you to pause and consider how you will respond to a situation rather than react habitually and negatively. The movement of the diaphragm during this type of breathing affects the vagus nerve which has a calming effect on your nervous system. Breathing like this is a useful first response when you notice your stress.

Driving in traffic is such a frequent example. If you are feeling irritated because traffic is slow or someone cuts in, just breathe, let go of muscular tension and try not to react. Reactions can escalate to road rage in people who do not recognise their negative emotions i.e. anger, and handle them appropriately.

Anger in traffic is often a result of previous stress which has not been resolved and which has a cumulative effect. Does road rage reduce a driver's competence and judgement? Staying calm and focussed while driving is obviously essential. But driver competence can also be impaired by lack of sleep, as well as alcohol and drugs, both legal and illegal. Maybe we need a campaign on 'mindful' driving!

Many other situations can cause us to feel irritated, nervous or anxious, including job interviews, dental and medical appointments, and the everyday demands of work and home life. Taking time to pause and focus on the breath, relax and maybe adding a smile (even if you don't feel like it!) can give you a worthwhile calming break. In fact, any time you pause could be called a 'nurture break' to contribute to self-care.

So become familiar with your emotions and reactions, recognise your early warning signs of stress and choose an appropriate strategy. I will share many ways to outsmart stress and enhance your health and wellbeing in the following chapters.

Something to think about

In this book I will be sharing many healthy choices which can contribute

to the health and wellbeing of our body, mind and spirit. Take time to reflect on your own lifestyle and recognise habits that may not be serving you well. If you wish to change or add anything different to your life, create SMART goals to help you achieve these.

S   -   Specific

M   -   Measurable

A   -   Achievable

R   -   Relevant

T   -   Timely

When you do want to achieve a goal, it is considered that visualising the achievement of the goal will assist you to reach it. However, you also need to visualise the journey towards the goal. This means focussing on the whole process including any setbacks or barriers which you need to overcome in order to reach the goal. Many athletes and performers use visualisation, also known as mental rehearsal, to fine-tune the excellence they hope to achieve. Apparently, visualisation activates the same part of the brain as actually doing the task. We already know that the brain cannot differentiate between an actual experience and remembering it or visualising it.

At the end of each chapter, I will pose three questions on which you might like to ponder. In this way, you may come to realise that you need to make some changes to really enjoy your longevity. I wish you well!

Chapter 2

❁

Is Laughter the Best Medicine?

Chapter 2
Is Laughter the Best Medicine?

> *"Laughter is to the soul what soap is to the body."*
> *— Proverb*

I would love to share with you my journey of discovery regarding the health benefits of laughter. With my interest in stress, I couldn't resist a seminar called 'Stress, Humour and Health' many years ago. Presented by Dr Shayne Yates and Patricia Cameron-Hill, the objective was to teach people about choosing a healthy lifestyle and managing stress. Humour was integral to the seminar because Patricia had terrific comic timing and was so funny. We laughed all day while we received all this excellent information.

At the end of the day I felt great because I had really experienced the benefits of laughter. I felt revitalised and had a sense of wellbeing. (Let's be truly honest here! At the end of some seminars, I am rather tired and brain-dead, even though the content has been worthwhile.) So after that experience, I attended their seminars several times over the years.

In fact, Shayne and Patricia were so successful, they had a cult following. They have published two books and numerous educational DVDs and very much focus on the value of using humour in everyday life to reduce stress and improve health and wellbeing.

Dr Patch Adams

Because I was on their mailing list, Shayne and Patricia informed me that Dr Patch Adams (the original Clown Doctor) was presenting a seminar in Melbourne which they sponsored. I attended this seminar with Patch, in which he focussed on how to bring more laughter into our lives so that we could enjoy the benefits.

A very unique and charismatic individual, Patch also spoke about the 'pain paradigm'. By this, he meant all the bad news that arrives daily on your television screens and in all forms of media – now available 24 hours a day. We literally have wall-to-wall bad news and Patch's advice was to avoid it, particularly if you were not well or your wellbeing was being undermined in any way. Watching all that bad news (which seems to become more graphic as each year goes by) will definitely not make you feel any better. Patch actually recommended having a 'news fast' if you are very challenged or stressed in some way, which is very good advice. Of course, the bad news helps you to realise how well off you are. If you are a very empathic person and sensitive to other people's distress and trauma, look for good news and share it!

The following year, I returned to Melbourne for a clown workshop and another unique experience with Patch. I saw him in his clown persona interacting with some residents in an aged care facility. Patch starting singing softly to a lady who seemed asleep in her bed. She woke up and started laughing with delight. I couldn't hear the song, but it must have been well chosen.

Within our group was a tall young man, long-haired, dressed in black and on roller blades. He wore a very tall top hat and was very interested in Patch's clowning abilities. Many years later I discovered that this young doctor had become a Professor of Integrated Medicine! Patch has visited Perth twice in the intervening years and continues to influence

health professionals about the health benefits of laughter and the benefits of a holistic approach to patient treatment and care.

At this time I was presenting workshops myself on managing stress and teaching adults a relaxation game called JelliTime™ to play with the kids in their lives. I gradually introduced more information about the benefits of laughter as well.

Laughter Yoga

In November 2000, Dr Madan Kataria and his wife, Madhuri, visited Perth, Western Australia. In 1995, in Mumbai, India, they had created Laughter Yoga. Madan had read about the very substantial health benefits of laughter so he decided to create a system that would allow people to laugh more.

Initially, early one morning in March 1995, Dr Kataria went down to a local park and invited people to come and join him to share jokes and funny stories to generate laughter and improve their health and wellbeing. Madan told us that he asked about a hundred people, but on that first morning there were only five people, including his wife, Madhuri. The jokes and funny stories worked quite well and the crowd grew daily. However, on day 10 the women who had come along said to Dr Kataria, "We are not coming anymore – the jokes are getting very nasty," so he realised that he would need to find some other way to generate the laughter.

Dr Kataria practised yoga and his wife, Madhuri, was a yoga teacher. He looked at yoga and laughter to see if there were any parallels. Madhuri suggested that deep breathing, based on yoga, be added and Madan realised that both deep breathing and laughter brought more oxygen into the body. This is how the activity got its name, however there is no need to wear a leotard or bring a mat to participate in Laughter Yoga, as it is only the deep breathing from yoga which is part of the process.

Madan also discovered that the brain cannot tell the difference between intentional or simulated laughter and genuine laughter. In a group situation, because laughter is contagious, the laughter becomes genuine.

> *"A day without laughter is a day wasted."*
> *— Charlie Chaplin*

Laughter Yoga consists of hand-clapping rhythms (you might recognise a cha-cha as Madan was a keen ballroom dancer), the deep breathing from yoga and playful laughter exercises. Led by a leader in a Laughter Club or in many different workplaces and locations, and with many different groups, the resulting health benefits of laughter have been well-researched.

The benefits of laughter

Laughter Yoga provides aerobic exercise, even if the participants are seated, and increases the oxygen supply to the brain. Laughter stimulates the internal organs and the activity of the diaphragm stimulates lymphatic flow. Laughter reduces stress and tension by reducing the levels of the stress hormone cortisol. When these levels are raised, the brain does not work as well, and neither does the immune system. As we know, chronic stress contributes to chronic disease, so regularly inviting laughter into your life to reduce cortisol levels is a very good reason to participate in Laughter Yoga.

Laughter provides a 'DOSE' of feel-good hormones. These include Dopamine - the pleasure hormone, Oxytocin - the cuddle or bonding hormone, Serotonin - the mood hormone, and Endorphins - which help us to feel good and relieve pain.

Laughter strengthens the immune system, not only by reducing cortisol levels, but by raising the levels of T cells and antibodies in the blood. Laughter lowers blood pressure, burns calories and stabilises blood sugar levels. Following a session of Laughter Yoga, the participants feel warmer due to the aerobic exercise, feel more awake and alert with an improved mood and sense of relaxation and wellbeing, which can persist for several hours. Laughter enhances relationships, wellbeing and productivity in the workplace, and it contributes to our resilience and the ability to bounce back from daily stress.

"We who laugh...last!" — LaughWA Inc.

Research on the benefits of laughter

Laughter has been recognised for many centuries as having a positive effect on body, mind and spirit. It was in 1979 that Norman Cousins, a renowned journalist and adjunct professor of psychiatry and behavioural science at UCLA in Los Angeles, published his book, *'Anatomy of an Illness, as perceived by the patient'*. The illness that he experienced occurred in 1964 and he eventually decided to share his story of reversing a significant immune system disease called Ankylosing Spondylitis. He did this by using the benefits of humour and other positive emotions to overcome it, as well as high doses of Vitamin C. He eventually transferred from a hospital to a hotel and spent time watching funny movies and television shows, such as Candid Camera and even some old Marx Brothers films. It worked!

"I made the joyous discovery that ten minutes of genuine belly laughter had an anaesthetic effect and would give me at least two hours of pain-free sleep." — Norman Cousins

This process did start in hospital and a nurse also read to him out of numerous humour books. However, as Norman was disturbing other patients with his laughter, arrangements were made for him to transfer to a hotel. His situation improved sufficiently for him to go back to his position as a full-time editor of the Saturday Review. Norman's account of his illness and recovery was attributed to the placebo effect and resulted in much discussion within the medical profession.

Scientists eventually became interested in researching the physiological changes and health benefits of laughter, which have resulted in numerous studies. These initial studies evaluated the effects of humour-induced laughter.

Laughter and cardiac function

Dr William Fry, a psychiatrist at Stanford University, California, demonstrated in the late 60's that most of the body's major physiological systems are stimulated by mirthful laughter. One of his studies confirmed that twenty seconds of intense laughter (even if 'faked') can double the heartrate for three to five minutes. It was proved that mirthful laughter provides aerobic exercise and can reduce the risk of respiratory infections. The positive cardio-vascular benefits of laughter continue to be identified.

Recent research has demonstrated that blood flow is decreased by 35% in subjects experiencing stress, whereas it is improved by 22% in subjects during laughter. It is possible that laughter may be important in reducing cardio-vascular disease, as these benefits were similar to those seen with aerobic activity but without the aches, pains and muscle tension of exercise. Stress and depression are now recognised as key factors in the development of cardio-vascular disease, as well as other lifestyle factors.

Dr Lee Berk, PhD, Loma Linda University Medical Centre, was inspired by Norman Cousins, and his team of researchers in the field of psycho-neuro-immunology (PNI) and studied the physical impact of mirthful laughter. In one study, heart attack patients were divided into two groups. One group was placed under standard medical care and the other half watched humorous videos for thirty minutes each day. After one year the 'humour' group had fewer arrhythmias, lower blood pressure, lower levels of stress hormones, and required lower doses of medication. The non-humour group had two and a half times more recurrent heart attacks than the humour group (50% vs 20%).

Humour induced laughter

All the initial research undertaken to examine the physiological effects and health benefits of laughter was based on laughter induced by humour. Whatever aspect was being tested, the subjects were divided into three groups. The first group watched a funny film or video, the second group watched a boring documentary, and there was no intervention for the third group. Various physiological parameters were measured before and afterwards. In this way, the increase of pain threshold was identified using the stimulus of icy water or a blood pressure cuff.

There was an increase in the immune response, and sustained laughter was found to have an aerobic effect and increasing oxygen uptake. As the years have gone by, there has been more sophisticated scientific research. Recent research by Dr Lee Berk using Magnetic Resonance Imaging (MRI) has demonstrated that the brain patterns of individuals who are expert meditators is very similar to that of a person who is experiencing sustained laughter. In effect, they are in a state of being totally present i.e. mindfulness.

Laughter in medical settings

Doctors and nurses have published numerous enthusiastic articles about the value of using gentle humour and laughter with their patients. Perceived benefits include:

- Establishing rapport with patients

- Reducing patient anxiety

- Improving compliance with treatment

- Enhancing relationships

- Reducing the stress of hospitalisation, procedures and treatments for both adults and children.

Dr Patch Adams is well known for promoting a holistic approach to patient care which does not just treat the disease. It involves the patient in a total caring relationship in which trust, compassion, fun, humour and laughter promote healing. Clown Doctors regularly contribute to the wellbeing of patients, families and staff in children's hospitals. In aged care facilities in Australia, Elder Clowns and Laughter Bosses, trained through the Humour Foundation, bring humour and playfulness to the residents, to engage them and contribute to their quality of life.

In the SMILE study, which was published in the BMJ Open 2013, professional 'Elder Clowns' provided 9-12 weekly humour therapy sessions, augmented by resident engagement by trained staff 'Laughter Bosses'. The controls received usual care. Those who participated had significantly reduced agitation without the side effects of medication. Professor Henry Brodaty was a key investigator and a documentary of the whole project was created called '*The Smile Within*' and shown on ABC Television.

Another research project was undertaken by nurses in the USA. It identified which complementary and alternative therapies were being accessed by women who were receiving orthodox medical treatment for breast cancer. As you might expect, nutrition, supplements, meditation, support groups and prayer were utilised. The surprising fact was that 21% of the women were using Humour and Laughter Therapy as part of their treatment regime.

Another article described a woman with breast cancer having chemotherapy while watching her favourite 'I Love Lucy' video and laughing heartily. What a wonderful way to reduce stress, prime her much needed immune system and switch on the positive physiology of healing!

Ros Ben-Moshe, a laughter therapist in Melbourne, has recently published a book called '*Laughing at cancer*'. She shares her moving and inspirational story of recovering from bowel cancer in her forties using love, laughter and mindfulness.

Laughter – a complementary therapy in the USA

The American Association of Therapeutic Humor has played a significant role in training Laughter Therapists and promoting the healing effects of laughter. Many major organisations which educate and support people with a range of chronic diseases recommend that they add laughter therapy to their health management. This was initially based on humour-induced laughter and was recommended for patients with diabetes, cancer, heart disease, multiple sclerosis, stroke, depression and Parkinson's, as an adjunct to conventional therapies. There is continual media coverage of the health benefits of laughter and in recent years, the research on the benefits of Laughter Yoga is becoming widely known.

Laughter Yoga research

Laughter Yoga is practised in 106 countries now and research is regularly published.

- **South Africa:** Dr Gita Suraj Narayan from the University of Kwazulu-Natal published her research in 2010 on the benefits of Laughter Yoga, which resulted in a reduction in post-stroke depression, enhanced mobility, reduction of pain intensity and improved communication and relations between the patient and significant others.

- **Australia:** Ros Ben-Moshe from Latrobe University introduced Laughter Yoga into a residential facility with such positive results that 92 staff were trained to introduce Laughter Yoga to all additional 30 facilities. The research was published in 2017.

- **Australia:** Associate Professor Paul Bennett from Deakin University initiated a research project to introduce Laughter Yoga into a Dialysis Unit in Victoria with positive outcomes for both the patients and staff. His research was published in 2015.

There has been increasing interest in the benefits of Laughter Yoga for older people, those in residential care, as well as those living with dementia and their carers.

- **Iran:** Laughter Yoga is at least as effective as group exercise programs in improvement of depression and life satisfaction of elderly depressed women. *International Journal of Geriatric Psychiatry (2010)*.

- **Korea:** Laughter Therapy is considered to be a useful, cost-effective and accessible intervention that has positive effects on depression, insomnia, and sleep quality in the elderly. *Geriatric Gerontology International (2011)*.

- **Japan:** The combination of a laughter and exercise program might have physiological and psychological health benefits for the elderly. Laughter might be an effective strategy to motivate the elderly to participate in physical activity. *Geriatric Gerontology International (2012)*.

- **America:** A research project conducted by Celeste Greene (LaughActive), in collaboration with The Gerontology Institute, Georgia State University, Atlanta, combined Laughter Yoga and physical activity for strength, balance and flexibility for older adults. Significant improvements were observed in mental health, aerobic endurance and self-efficacy in the participants, by eliciting positive emotions through laughter as part of the exercise program. *The Gerontologist (2016)*.

The Potential of Laughter Yoga

As a physiotherapist, who has been promoting, sharing and advocating for the benefits of Laughter Yoga for nearly 17 years, I am well aware of the potential of enhancing exercise and rehabilitation programs by adding Laughter Yoga to them. In 2015, as a member of The Australian Association of Gerontology, I submitted an abstract to their annual conference which was to be held in November in Alice Springs, the Red Centre of Australia! My abstract, which was called 'Laughter Therapy – Potential for Improvement in Health and Wellbeing', was accepted for a poster presentation.

The abstract details some of the less pleasant consequences of ageing, but I will address these in a future chapter. It also presented the history of Laughter Therapy and the information about research which I have already shared with you. It gave an overview of Laughter Yoga and the many individuals and organisations in Western Australia which have

experienced its benefits. These have included health professionals, people of all ages with disabilities and other chronic conditions, members of the Aboriginal community and those working in aged care, mental health, education and the corporate world.

The trip to Alice Springs was memorable and resulted in an invitation from Blue Cross, an Aged Care Provider in Melbourne, to present a two-hour workshop for their lifestyle coordinators, which introduced them to Laughter Yoga. The key principles guiding the staff at Blue Cross include: **Be There, Make Their Day, Choose Your Attitude, and Have Fun!**

Advocacy for Laughter Yoga

In 2016 I had the pleasure of sharing Laughter Yoga with 150 physiotherapists at a Symposium at the University of Western Australia (UWA) Club with an enthusiastic response, positive feedback and increased interest in the potential of Laughter Yoga. I was also invited to share Laughter Yoga with all 250 staff of Therapy Focus, an organisation which provides services to children with developmental delays or disability and their families. This was a major awards event for the staff and the Laughter Yoga was fully embraced, raising the mood and connecting the participants.

This year I have submitted another abstract to the Annual Conference of The Australian Gerontology Association which fortunately is being held in my home town of Perth, Western Australia. This time it is called 'Is Laughter Therapy a life-enhancing Golden Opportunity?' I am delighted to say that this abstract has just been accepted. I will have the opportunity to share Laughter Yoga with the delegates so that they can experience for themselves the instant positive benefits previously discussed. I hope that they will discover the relevance of including Laughter Therapy as

an effective activity in aged care. Laughter Yoga connects people in a group, giving them a sense of belonging and reducing their isolation. Surely all these benefits could enhance the function and quality of life of older people. If they are more awake and alert with an enhanced mood, perhaps they will be more aware and less at risk of having falls!

I am continually advocating to share these benefits and feel that this is my purpose in life!

How often do you laugh?

_____

Have you experienced Laughter Yoga?

_____

Is there a Laughter Club in your vicinity?

_____

> "If laughter cannot solve your problems, it will definitely DISSOLVE your problems; so that you can think clearly what to do about them." — Dr Madan Kataria

Chapter 3

❀

The Laughter Prescription

LAUGHTER
is the best
MEDICINE!

Chapter 3
The Laughter Prescription

> *"Love who you are and what you are and what you do. Laugh at yourself and at life and nothing can touch you."* — Louise Hay

If laughter is the best medicine, perhaps we need a prescription so that we understand the dosage, how to take the medicine, the benefits and side effects, if any. I created a Laughter Prescription many years ago and I would like to share it with you. You can also find a copy to download on my website (www.jannigoss.com) but for now I will lead you through it.

Laughter Prescription

**Optimal Daily Dosage:
20 minutes of Laughter**

- Share your Smile!
- Avoid Bad News. Look for Good News.
- Play, Laugh and have Fun with the People in Your Life, especially Children.
- Access more Comedy - TV, Movies, DVDs, Radio, Print Media and Internet.
- Be an Optimist - Have Hope in Your Life.
- Exercise Your Sense of Humour!
- Use Humour to De-Stress. Laugh at Yourself.
- Find a Laughter Club & do Laughter Yoga!
- Seek help if Laughter is elusive.
- Give Thanks for the Benefits of Laughter!

www.jannigoss.com

© Janni Goss

The optimal daily dosage is 20 minutes of laughter. Of course, for maximum benefit it is best for this to occur in one large dose. However, if you laugh regularly during the day, this is beneficial as well.

- **Share your Smile!**

    Let us start with smiling, which is how we can connect with each other. Because of our mirror neurones, we tend to mimic the facial expressions and gestures of the people we meet. This process helped our ancestors to determine who was friend and who was foe, and operates in our brains in the same way. The good news is that if you put a smile on your face, even though you don't feel like it, your brain thinks you are really smiling and provides endorphins anyway. So it is worth smiling at others because you will stimulate their mirror neurons, resulting in a smile and similar benefits. Smiling can be the precursor to laughter, engaging trust and connection and shared enjoyment. Just for fun, I provide smiling lessons in my presentations:

    Lesson 1: Place your index and middle fingers together, pointing to the ceiling, and with them gently stroke upwards at the corners of your mouth. You will be stimulating the muscles that turn the corners of your mouth up when you smile naturally. If you share this activity with anyone else, ask them to observe if anyone's corners are turning up! This request usually results in genuine smiles!

    Lesson 2: Take a straw or chopstick and place it between your teeth without closing your lips. Can you feel how this stretches your mouth sideways into a 'sort of' smiling position? However, it is not a true smile unless the corners are turning up and you are doing the crinkly bit with your eyes! Look around at others and see if they are really smiling.

If you do these lessons on your own, do them in front of a mirror, or just decide to put a smile on your face and notice how it enhances your appearance. Your smile is your best accessory!

> *"Wrinkles merely indicate where smiles have been."* — Mark Twain

- **Avoid Bad News. Look for Good News.**

As mentioned previously, Dr Patch Adams recommends reducing your access to bad news. If you have children in your life, be very vigilant about the news that they see or overhear. Radio news broadcasts often include graphic details not suitable for children's ears. Children may be traumatised by images on television and may misinterpret them. I was once told by a mother that her 8 year old son saw a bushfire on television which was in another state, however he became fearful that their house would burn down. Unfortunately, the emphasis on broadcasting all the dramas, tragedies, natural disasters, conflicts and wars creates a very negative impression of our world, which may affect children deeply.

Look for good news at www.thegoodnewsnetwork.org

- **Play, Laugh and have Fun with the People in Your Life, especially Children.**

This is the first way to get more laughter into your life. According to Dr Patch Adams, laughter is the social glue that binds us together. Take a look at all the people in your life with whom you interact. This is where the potential is to use your sense

of humour, share positive and amusing stories and include fun and laughter, particularly with the children in your life. Young children are playful and spontaneous. Their laughter is one of the most joyful sounds in the world. So if you have young children in your life, make the most of the opportunities to engage them in play. Physical play is important for all children and teenagers and reducing screen time is a significant priority.

You may have other family members, friends, neighbours and work colleagues with whom you can share laughter as well. I like to ban discussion of bad news in social situations, so that the time is well spent.

- **Access more Comedy – TV, Movies, DVDs, Radio, Print Media and Internet.**

This is the second way to invite more laughter into your life. It is the basis of Laughter Therapy as practised in America and recommended by the American Association of Therapeutic Humour (AATH). The challenge is to do some research to identify the style of humour that really makes you laugh. In fact, in America you can do an online Sense of Humour test (SOH) so that they can recommend appropriate humorous material for you.

I suggest that you discuss your favourite forms of humour with someone, and then do some research in libraries or video stores or online to identify your favourite style of humour. Perhaps you already have humorous TV series, movies or other programs on DVD at home. You can check your television program for re-runs of your favourite American or British sitcoms or current comedians and panel shows.

The idea is to do your own Laughter Therapy by choosing to watch half an hour of comedy at times when you need to revitalise yourself, improve your mood or share some fun with your nearest and dearest. When you get home from work may be a good time for a dose of therapeutic laughter to diminish the concerns and stress of your working day. Most of us have evening responsibilities as well, and having a good laugh may just help them to be more easily achievable. The internet is also a source of much comedic material and YouTube has much to offer, including amusing cat videos, which are popular!

- **Be an Optimist – Have Hope in Your Life.**

We are encouraged to be optimists and there is good evidence that optimists live longer and have happier lives. Learning strategies to improve one's wellbeing is time well spent. Laughter is a natural ingredient which also contributes to life's quality, and always having something to look forward to, such as a holiday, birthday, catching up with friends or achieving one's goals, adds to the pleasures of life. Hope gives meaning to life as we look forward to positive outcomes.

- **Exercise Your Sense of Humour!**

Our sense of humour is a very valuable asset. It allows us to see the funny side of life, the silver linings and contributes to our resilience. The resulting laughter reduces our stress and tension and helps us to bounce back from the challenges that life provides us.

- **Use Humour to De-Stress. Laugh at Yourself.**

Many occupations and professions are challenging. Doctors, nurses, paramedics, military personnel and first responders rely on their sense of humour to survive. The humour that they utilise in the workplace is often dark and appropriate only

to their own circumstances, which often involve trauma and challenge. As an example, I once read of a young doctor in London Hospital who used the term CTP to describe a patient's condition. Medical personnel often use shortened terminology and CTP meant 'circling the plughole', which meant that the patient was dying. This was graphic terminology but didn't offend anyone!

Can you laugh at yourself? This again is a positive sign of resilience. We all forget things, lose things and can't remember names, usually because we are not totally present or trying to multi-task instead of focussing on one thing at a time. This happens to people of all ages and is not unique to seniors! The term 'senior moment' has been superseded by the term 'intellectual interlude', which is somehow less derogatory. The good news is that as you get older, you have more opportunities to laugh at yourself. Indeed, if your reaction to these 'interludes' is to be self-critical, frustrated, irritated or angry, you are just generating negative emotions which are harmful to your health. So next time you have an 'intellectual interlude', try laughing, even if it is not genuine to start with – much better for your health!

- **Find a Laughter Club and do Laughter Yoga!**

Finally we arrive at the third major way to invite more laughter into your life. You can find Laughter Clubs online and the best outcomes occur if you attend regularly.

During a Laughter Yoga session for adults, they may participate either standing or sitting. The following principles are observed:

- Each individual is asked to take responsibility for their own health and wellbeing, pacing themselves and not causing any discomfort, as Laughter Yoga is an aerobic activity.

Precautions are recommended by Dr Kataria as Laughter Yoga is aerobic exercise. People with the following conditions are advised to check with their doctor before doing laughter exercises regularly. These include hernia, any conditions involving bleeding i.e. piles, heart problems with chest pain, following major surgeries, epilepsy and severe backache. Pregnant women who have a history of miscarriage are advised not to participate. Do not attend a Laughter Club if you have a cold or flu and spread it around!

I like to suggest that if anyone is stiff or sore anywhere, to move carefully and not cause any new pain. They can pace themselves, rest or sit down if they need to – it is their responsibility.

- The participants make lots of eye contact, which helps them connect, interact and generate the laughter.

- Laughing only – no talking. The facilitator is the only person who speaks. This can be a challenge for some people!

- Act out the laughter exercises using your imagination and creativity, and trust the process! This is an opportunity to rediscover your playfulness!

- Above all, be enthusiastic!

I have already shared the history of Laughter Yoga with you so now I will share the process. The following components of Laughter Yoga are:

CLAPPING   Clap so both hands are in full contact, moving them from side to side.

Ho! Ho! Ha! Ha! Ha! Do this four times.

Clapping is used to mark the end of each laughter exercise and is intermittently followed by three deep breaths, which are based on yoga. It may feel a little strange to go Ho! Ho! Ha! Ha! Ha! You are in fact using the same muscles as if you were really laughing, so your brain takes notice!

BREATHING   Raise your arms as you breathe in fully, hold and stretch, then breathe out slowly through your mouth so it takes twice as long to breathe out. Repeat twice. The third time, laugh the air out!

PLAY   To create an attitude of playfulness (often missing in our serious adult life) clap hands together twice, saying:

Very Good! (clap) Very Good! (clap) Yeeaay! (with arms and thumbs up).

Repeat twice. This device is used frequently during the process. This mantra can be used at other times in your life to acknowledge other people's success, especially when you catch your kids doing something right!

GREETINGS The session starts with a greeting. Participants move around and can use a variety of greetings accompanied by laughter only.

Namaste (an Indian greeting with hands held together in a prayer position which means 'you and I are one')

Hand Shake (laugh a greeting – this is what we call 'intentional laughter' and it can become genuine as Laughter Yoga proceeds.)

Electric Hand Shake (as if receiving an electric current!)

LAUGHTER EXERCISES – There are literally hundreds of laughter exercises which use imagination, creativity, playfulness, everyday events, scenarios and themes to generate the laughter. Initially, the laughter is intentional – that is, we decide to laugh, but during the process, because of the contagious nature of laughter, we discover genuine laughter. There are many variations on the clapping mantras and breathing exercises and the process lasts for about 25-30 minutes. During a presentation, the Laughter Yoga may only last 15 minutes, but this is sufficient time for the participants to experience the immediate benefits. At a Laughter Club we conclude with a Laughter Meditation and some final rituals.

LAUGHTER MEDITATION – For this meditation, we may choose to sit in a circle on the floor and initiate laughter with a smile, a giggle and increasing laughter which becomes real. Those who laugh easily or have an interesting laugh are great

value. For some people, their laughter gets out of control and is full of snorts and cackles which triggers other people's laughter! We can then lie down and let the laughter take over. It may come and go in waves but this is what Dr Kataria calls, "Laughing for no reason." This is when we can experience the full intensity of laughter. When the laughter subsides we spend some time enjoying how we feel and the sensation of wellbeing which laughter brings. A guided meditation may be included. By moving our hands and feet and breathing in fully with a big stretch, we come back to reality, slowly rolling onto the side before coming up to sitting. I then like to ask people if they are feeling different in some way to the start of the session and identify the benefits of laughter which I share with them. For the final ritual at a Laughter Club, we spend a minute contemplating or silently praying for World Peace. The Leader then asks three questions to which the participants reply enthusiastically, "WE ARE!"

1. Who are the luckiest people in the world? "WE ARE!"

2. Who are the happiest/healthiest people in the world? "WE ARE!"

3. Who is going to add more Laughter to their lives? "WE ARE!"

The third question can be adapted to be relevant to particular groups or audiences.

- **Seek help if Laughter is elusive.**

There is no doubt that having an active and available Sense of Humour (SOH) is a great asset in everyday life. However, there are times when negative emotions predominate because of life stress, to the point that our SOH disappears, also known as a 'humorectomy'! As for me, if I find myself in a challenging situation in which my SOH has deserted me, this is a very

serious matter! Losing one's SOH is an early warning sign of significant stress and indicates that steps needs to be taken to remedy the situation.

- **Give Thanks for the Benefits of Laughter!**

As we have said previously, research has demonstrated the physiological and psychological benefits of laughter, as well as the positive influence on social and spiritual wellbeing. The following benefits of laughter are easy to recognise and remember, so please share them widely. We are designed to be amused, to be playful, and to experience joy and happiness. This is a great gift to the human race!

The wonderful thing about Laughter Yoga is that it is accessible to everyone regardless of race, culture, language, beliefs, gender, age or abilities. In spite of our perceived differences, we are all more the same than we are different, and we all laugh in the same language!

Dr Kataria believes that Laughter Yoga contributes to good health, joy and peace in the world. On World Laughter Day, which is held on the first Sunday in May each year, the members of all the Laughter Clubs around the globe in 106 countries invite members of their communities to enjoy Laughter Yoga and share our united desire for World Peace.

Enjoy the benefits which follow and you can also download them from my website: www.jannigoss.com.

THE BENEFITS OF LAUGHTER

- Provides aerobic exercise & increases the oxygen supply to the brain.

- Relieves stress & tension & lowers cortisol levels. *(stress hormone)*

- Lowers blood pressure & produces a feeling of relaxation & well-being.

- Burns calories & stabilizes blood sugar levels.

- Strengthens the Immune system.

- Provides a D.O.S.E. of happy hormones - Dopamine, Oxytocin, Seratonin & Endorphins which improve your mood & can relieve pain.

- Enhances relationships & can boost productivity in the workplace.

- Starting with each individual, Laughter Yoga may eventually contribute to World Peace.

Ho! Ho! Ha! Ha! Ha!

Janni Goss B.App.Sci(Physio)
Laughter Ambassador
Laughter Yoga International
Perth, Western Australia

www.jannigoss.com

Here in Western Australia, Laughter Yoga has been a significant part of my life since November 2000. The Perth Laughter Club, initiated by Grant Stone, is one of the longest running Laughter Clubs in Australia and meets fortnightly at the Loftus Centre in Leederville. I have had three Laughter Clubs which are usually named for the suburb in which they are held. These were Shenton Park, Cottesloe at the Cancer Wellness Centre, and Belmont at the local library. We have a not-for-profit organisation called LaughWA Inc. which was also initiated by Grant. It has been crucial in providing Laughter Yoga Trainings, supporting Laughter Clubs and creating an enthusiastic Laughter Community here in Western Australia. You can find out all about us, Laughter Clubs, Trainings and Events at www.laughwa.org.au

There are multiple resources on the internet including articles, videos, online trainings, Laughter Conferences and Facebook pages. Please see the resources page for details.

When was the last time you laughed so hard that you had tears in your eyes?

_____

_____

Do you laugh more at home or at work?

_____

_____

What is your favourite style of comedy and when can you access it?

_____

_____

> "Laughter is the sun that drives winter from the human face." — Victor Hugo

Chapter 4

❀

The Science of Wellbeing

Chapter 4
The Science of Wellbeing

> *"The most important relationship in my life is the one with myself." — Anon*

There has been much scientific enquiry and discussion regarding the terms happiness, wellbeing and wellness. According to people's interpretation, each term has a unique meaning but they overlap as well, as you will see from all the following viewpoints.

Happiness

His Holiness, The Dalai Lama, teaches us that our purpose in life is to be happy. However, we will not achieve happiness unless we relieve the suffering of others and help them to be happy. This Buddhist philosophy encourages loving kindness, empathy, compassion and altruism in the form of service to others.

Seven Dimensions of Wellness

The University of California Riverside has published Seven Dimensions of Wellness which is the model of wellness used on their campus and includes:

- Social Wellness – the ability to relate and connect with others and to establish and maintain positive relationships with family, friends and co-workers.

- Emotional Wellness – the ability to understand ourselves and cope with the challenges life can bring, acknowledging and sharing feelings of anger, fear, sadness or stress, as well as hope, love, joy and happiness.

- Spiritual Wellness – the ability to establish peace and harmony in our lives by developing congruency between values and actions to achieve a common purpose.

- Environmental Wellness – the ability to recognise our own responsibility on the quality of air, water and land, making a positive impact on the quality of our environment and the planet.

- Occupational Wellness – the ability to achieve personal fulfilment from our occupations and careers while maintaining balance in our lives.

- Intellectual Wellness – the ability to be open to new ideas and experiences, which affect personal decisions, group interaction, community improvement and committing to lifelong learning.

- Physical Wellness – the ability to maintain a healthy quality of life which allows us to achieve our daily activities without undue fatigue or physical stress. There is a need to recognise behaviours which impact on our wellness so that we adopt healthy habits and avoid destructive ones.

This is a very useful and comprehensive view of wellness, but I can't help wondering whether these dimensions also include Academic Wellness, Financial Wellness and Sexual Wellness, all very relevant on a university campus!

Positive Psychology – Happiness and Wellbeing

Dr Martin Seligman, who is the creator of Positive Psychology, has done a great deal of research on happiness and wellbeing. His initial findings on happiness demonstrated that many people equate this state with meeting their needs at some time in the future. For instance, people may say that they will be happy when:

- They win Lotto!

- Christmas comes or, for some, when Christmas is over!

- They have paid off their mortgage!

- They have finished their studies!

- They get a better job!

- They retire!

- They lose five kilos!

- They go on that cruise!

- They find the love of their life!

Dr Seligman determined that what we really need is to find a sense of wellbeing here and now in the present moment, not wait for some future event to provide our happiness. His research resulted in him naming five pillars of wellbeing, which are contained in the letters:

PERMA

Positive Emotions

Engagement

Relationships

Meaning

Accomplishment

As we know, psychologists are trained to assist us to deal with the problems that we encounter in life which we cannot solve on our own. They use many strategies and therapies to help us reduce our stress, overcome anxiety, depression, loss and grief, as well as to relinquish unhealthy habits and addictions. Dr Seligman believed that it might be more effective to identify an individual's character strengths and build on those, so that they became more resilient and are better equipped to deal with stressful life events. His research demonstrated the five pillars of wellbeing which PERMA represents.

P   POSITIVE EMOTIONS are the first pillar of wellbeing. They include love, gratitude, empathy, kindness, compassion, joy, contentment, pleasure, wonder and amusement. Seligman's research on the impact of gratitude demonstrated that by writing down three events that went well during the day (What Went Well – 'www') each evening at bedtime, people's outlook on life improved over several months. This practice is regularly recommended to help people focus on the more positive and enjoyable events of the day, rather than dwell on any negative aspects of the day. Additional positive emotions are self-esteem and optimism.

E ENGAGEMENT is about flow and losing track of time during an absorbing activity. It means being totally involved in the task at hand, with purpose and commitment.

R POSITIVE RELATIONSHIPS with other people are the best antidote to the ups and downs of life and contribute to our longevity. Science has found that we do not thrive on isolation and doing a kindness for someone else is the most reliable way to increase our sense of wellbeing.

M MEANING pertains to belonging to and serving that which we believe is bigger than ourselves. Meaning is often pursued for its own sake and provides motivation and commitment to persist in our beliefs and actions.

A ACCOMPLISHMENT relates to what we achieve in our lives. The elements of achievement are based on the theory that achievement equals skill x effort. Acknowledging and celebrating our achievements contributes to our wellbeing.

Laughter Yoga and PERMA

For me, Laughter Yoga has definitely provided the five pillars of wellbeing. I share positive emotions and positive relationships with the members of my Laughter Community every time we share a Laughter Club, Committee Meeting or Training. At every presentation, I experience the benefits of laughter myself when sharing Laughter Yoga and the positive response of my audience is a reward worth celebrating!

When engaged in Laughter Yoga, I feel totally focussed and involved, which I guess puts me in a state of flow.

Because I share Dr Kataria's vision of contributing to other people's good health and joy, as well as the potential for World Peace, this gives

meaning to my contributions. I sincerely believe that Laughter Yoga could make a big difference to older people if health professionals accepted it as a form of Laughter Therapy, so I will continue to network and use every opportunity to advocate for its inclusion in the Health and Ageing sector.

Character strengths

In his book, *'Flourish'* (2011), Dr Seligman gives the full history of his journey with Positive Psychology, his extensive research and how its principles and theories have been successfully utilised in many domains. Positive Psychology has been introduced into numerous educational institutions in the USA and here in Australia. It is part of the training of the military in America to improve resilience and reduce post-traumatic stress disorder (PTSD).

Dr Seligman developed a list of 24 signature strengths, which you can find in an appendix in *'Flourish'*. There is also a complete questionnaire on his website with which you can evaluate your own character strengths: www.authentichappiness.org

There are six categories with additional items which are listed below:

- Wisdom and Knowledge
    - Curiosity, Love of Learning, Judgement, Ingenuity, Social Intelligence, Perspective
- Courage
    - Valour, Perseverance, Integrity
- Humanity and Love
    - Kindness, Loving
- Justice
    - Citizenship, Fairness, Leadership

- Temperance

    - Self-control, Prudence, Humility

- Transcendence

    - Appreciation of Beauty, Gratitude, Hope, Spirituality, Forgiveness, Humour, Zest

The list of all the strengths is much more detailed in the book and online with very specific statements which you can score. For example:

"I treat all people equally, regardless of who they might be" is…

- Very much like me   5

- Like me   4

- Neutral   3

- Unlike me   2

- Very much unlike me   1

By scoring all the statements, you can identify your own strengths and those which you may be able to improve.

This test was originally published in '*Authentic Happiness*' in 2002 and provides insight into one's attitudes, beliefs and values.

Wellbeing – Wellness

Professor Marc Cohen of RMIT Melbourne has a long and successful career focussing on integrative medicine, research and the parameters for health and wellbeing. He was in fact the young doctor in the top hat on rollerblades who accompanied Dr Patch Adams on his visit to

a nursing home. Maybe this encounter had a profound effect! In an article published in 2001, he wrote that the medical profession's focus on dealing with negative mental states has led to the suggestion of classifying 'happiness' as a major affective disorder (pleasant type). He described the symptoms and signs of happiness and discussed its health benefits. Epidemiological data suggested that happiness is related to personality factors such as high self-esteem, feelings of personal control and extroversion and is unrelated to demographic factors or the ownership of consumer goods. Humour is a communication device specifically designed to elicit joy and happiness and is effective in relieving anxiety and stress and enhances communication in medical settings. Recapturing the optimistic enchantment with life that is a part of childhood may be a key to happiness and health.

Play is also an integral part of childhood and Laughter Yoga provides us with the opportunity to rediscover our playfulness!

Professor Cohen also shared some research results which demonstrated that being loved increases longevity. Two groups of rabbits were fed identical unhealthy diets to challenge their ability to survive. Surprisingly, one group lived much longer than the other, which really puzzled the researchers who had set up identical protocols. They then discovered that the person caring for the surviving rabbits had spent time patting and nurturing them when they were fed, and this contributed to their longevity!

Vitamin L stands for giving and receiving Love and is integral to our wellbeing!

Vitamin F stands for Friends with whom we share the ups and downs of life, the celebrations and commiserations, giving support to each other and just being there as good listeners.

Vitamin P stands for Pets! Research demonstrates the differences between dog and cat owners. Dog owners are considered to be more extrovert and fitter as they take their dogs for a walk. They socialise with other dog owners and really appreciate the companionship, faithfulness and unconditional love of their canine friend.

On the other hand, cat owners are said to be more sensitive, creative and introverted, and really appreciate the affection of their cat. In fact, owning a cat or being owned by a cat, is beneficial for your health as it reduces the risk of stroke. Cats give you a great example of how to relax and if you spend time stroking your cat, you relax as well and your blood pressure drops.

If you happen to have two different pets, you are known as 'bi-petual' – which needs to be said carefully!

Social and Emotional Wellbeing (SEWB)

Within the Aboriginal and Torres Strait Islander community, the concept of health is holistic. SEWB is defined as a multi-dimensional concept of health that includes mental health, but also encompasses connection to land or 'country', culture, spirituality, ancestry, family and community. Aboriginal health does not just mean the physical wellbeing of an individual, but refers to the social, emotional and cultural wellbeing of the whole community, for which there are nine guiding principles:

1. Health as holistic

2. The right to self-determination

3. The need for cultural understanding

4. The impact of history in trauma and loss

5. Recognition of human rights

6. The impact of racism and stigma

7. Recognition of the centrality of kinship

8. Recognition of cultural diversity

9. Recognition of Aboriginal strengths

SEWB, from an Aboriginal and Torres Strait Islander's perspective, involves connection to body, to mind and emotions, to family and kinship, to community, to culture, to country, and to spirit, spirituality and ancestors. Respect and cultural safety are paramount.

On the many occasions that I have shared Laughter Yoga with members of the Aboriginal community, they have totally embraced the opportunity to play and laugh. Their ability to laugh at whatever life delivers to them has been central to their survival!

Five daily activities to enhance wellbeing

Dr Nic Marks, founder of the Centre for Wellbeing at the UK think tank New Economics Foundation (NEF), gathers evidence about what makes us happy. He is particularly keen to promote a balance between sustainable development and quality of life. He devised the Happy Planet Index, a global index of human wellbeing and environmental impact. The results indicated that people in the world's wealthiest countries who consumed most of the planet's resources don't come out on top in terms of wellbeing. However, the Kingdom of Bhutan uses Gross National Happiness as a significant indicator of economic and social wellbeing.

Dr Marks' research discovered that, as well as gratitude, which is thought to be the foundation of wellbeing, there are five more ways to enhance wellbeing:

CONNECT   Isolation is not good for us, so the more social connections and interactions we have with family, friends, neighbours, colleagues, etc., the more our life will be supported and enriched every day.

BE ACTIVE   Movement and physical activity are essential to our health, and the best exercise is the one that you actually do! Go for a walk, play a game or sport, swim, garden and laugh to help you feel good. Discover an activity that you enjoy and suits your level of mobility and fitness. Try dancing!

TAKE NOTICE   Be aware of the world around you and be curious. Notice what is beautiful, unusual, intriguing, delicious, the changing seasons, your own feelings and sensations, and appreciate it all. Be mindful. This ties in with experiencing gratitude and **'Taking in the Good'**!

KEEP LEARNING   Lifelong learning is recommended, so try something new, rediscover an old interest, learn a new language, skill or hobby, and use the internet. Challenge yourself and enjoy the fun, the achievement and the increased confidence. Your brain will appreciate these opportunities to create new neurons and connections, building your cognitive reserve.

GIVE   Altruism, generosity and service, combined with kindness and compassion, such as in volunteering, sharing your smile or joining a community group will reward you. When you give, you also receive.

Well, I have given you plenty to think about and I hope you find it useful to make the most of your wellbeing!

What activities do you choose to do to enhance your wellbeing?

_____

_____

What are you grateful for in your life?

_____

_____

If you have a pet, what benefits do you experience?

_____

_____

"Attitude is a choice. Happiness is a choice.
Optimism is a choice. Kindness is a choice. Giving is a choice.
Respect is a choice. Whatever choice you make, makes you.
Choose wisely." — Roy T. Bennett

Chapter 5

❀

More Strategies to Outsmart Stress

Less Stress
Just Ahead

Chapter 5
More Strategies to Outsmart Stress

> "In today's rush we all think too much, seek too much, want too much and forget about the joy of just being." — Eckhart Tolle

The first strategy that I shared with you, was to breathe slowly in response to a stressful situation in order to calm your nervous system, and I would like to discuss this further.

Breathing

Sometimes our breathing becomes shallow due to stress, anxiety, tension or poor posture. When you become aware of this, use your breath to increase your oxygen supply, decrease tension and calm yourself. We need to be aware that sitting for long periods of time can affect our posture and breathing pattern and is certainly not recommended, as we are designed to move regularly.

You can try out the following breathing techniques and see which one works best for you. Sit comfortably in a chair with your back well supported or, if appropriate, lie down.

- Breathe in fully, hold for a count of 4 then breathe out slowly through your mouth, so it takes twice as long to breathe out. Repeat twice only.

- You can also raise your arms above your head as you breathe

in fully, have a gentle stretch and then lower your arms as you exhale, taking twice as long to breathe out. Repeat twice only. This is the same yoga breath that is used in Laughter Yoga.

- Breathe at your normal rate, in and out through your nose. Notice the temperature of the air as you breathe in and breathe out, and notice if it feels different. This focus on your breath is a form of mindfulness and helps to quieten your mind when it gets busy. If you have trouble noticing the difference in the temperature, place your index finger beneath your nostrils and continue to breathe. You will notice a difference then!

- Breathe at your normal rate, in through your nose, out through your mouth. As you breathe in, imagine oxygen and energy entering your body and as you exhale, breathe out any tension left in your body. Continue for as long as it takes to feel calm and relaxed, maybe only a few minutes.

- Breathe at your normal rate. As you breathe in, say to yourself, "calm" and as you exhale, say, "and peaceful." Continue for as long as it takes to feel calm and relaxed.

- Finally, you can breathe in for a count of 4, hold the breath for a count of 7, and exhale for a count of 8. As you breathe out, place the tip of your tongue on the gum behind your upper front teeth. Initially do this only three times, but gradually increase. This breathing technique was devised by Dr Andrew Weil.

As you focus on your breath and body, you can reduce tension and calm your mind. It is a form of mindfulness. Even a few minutes of breathing can calm your nervous system, change how you feel and give you a nurture break. It may also help you get to sleep at night.

My Story

Many years ago my car broke down on a six lane highway. I climbed over a fence to knock on the door of an adjacent house in order to summon some help (pre-mobile phone days). Then I went and sat in the car and waited. It was a red car, the hazard lights were on and the bonnet was up. Unfortunately, a distracted truck driver failed to observe my car and drove straight into it. As he approached from behind, I gradually realised that he was not going to change lanes! As you can imagine, I thought this was the end of me. However, I survived, although the car didn't. When I started driving again, whenever I saw a truck in the rear vision mirror, my fight and flight response would be triggered. In fact, it was actually a freeze response and I would stop breathing! I literally had to force myself to take some slow breaths. Over time, I found that I no longer had a stress response when driving and in fact, I enjoy driving, but do so mindfully! This is the power of the breath!

Mindfulness – calming the nervous system

Mindfulness, which is a state of being totally present and focussed in the here and now, without being judgemental, is highly recommended for its many benefits. We are often distracted by past concerns or future worries which diminish our presence and enjoyment in the present moment. By being mindful, we can enjoy life's simple pleasures more easily. As an example, mindful shopping, food preparation and eating can enhance the pleasure of eating and sharing food. You can be mindful of making healthy choices while shopping, enjoy the colour, texture, aroma and taste as you prepare and then mindfully eat your meal. Eating a rainbow of fruit and vegetables can be a multi-sensory experience if we are truly present!

Mindfulness meditation is an extension of this concept. By focussing on your breathing while seated in an upright position or even lying down, it is possible to be totally present and not engage with the thoughts that

may arise. They can just pass you by like clouds in the sky. Learning meditation allows us to become more attentive, aware and present. It can also calm our nervous system and help us to be less reactive, so that we respond thoughtfully to what is occurring around us, rather than out of habit. This, of course, involves emotional intelligence, which is the ability to recognise our own emotions and respond appropriately to them, as well as to other people's emotions. If we are less reactive, we will respond more calmly to what life delivers to us and can be more creative in finding solutions.

The good news is that laughter also creates a state of mindfulness and is the quickest and easiest way to reduce the effects of stress, boost our immune system and contribute to health and wellbeing.

Significant teachers

There are so many resources available to help you to understand and learn the techniques of mindfulness meditation. You may find local classes, courses online or many books which are available by authors such as Jon Kabat-Zinn Ph.D. who initially combined the philosophies of western psychology with eastern philosophy to create Mindfulness-Based Stress Reduction (MBSR) techniques. His book is called '*Full Catastrophe Living – Using the Wisdom of Your Body and Mind to Face Stress, Pain, and Illness*' and was reissued in 2009.

Other significant teachers of mindfulness include Thich Nhat Hanh, a Vietnamese Buddhist Monk, who has taught and inspired many people to embrace mindfulness and other Buddhist principles.

Dr Ian Gawler has been a strong advocate for the health benefits of mindfulness meditation, especially in dealing with chronic health problems, including cancer, which he has personally survived.

David Michie is another experienced meditation teacher who has written several books on the subject, including three delightful novels from the point of view of a cat who happens to have been rescued by the Dalai

Lama. During the time that she spends with her master, she listens to all the conversations and teachings that the Dalai Lama shares with his visitors. *'The Dalai Lama's Cat'* provides us with insights on how to find happiness and meaning in a busy, materialistic world. The second novel, *'The Art of Purring'*, discusses the vital subject of happiness. The third novel, *'The Power of Meow'*, expands the cat's understanding of being mindful. Many insights can be gained from reading these delightful, whimsical tales! Interestingly, David has also written a book called *'Mindfulness is Better than Chocolate'*.

These are just a few examples of highly-acclaimed teachers and their work, which is easily available on their websites, in bookshops or online.

Should you need any persuasion that adding mindfulness and meditation to your life is a good idea, some of the benefits are listed below, which have been provided from the work of David Michie.

NOTES ON MEDITATION

Mindfulness is the practice of paying attention to the present moment on purpose and non-judgementally – that is, *being* rather than always *doing*. Mindfulness training is becoming rapidly adopted in fields as diverse as business, sports, education, the military, and the justice and health care systems.

Clinical trials, as well as extensive experience, show that the practice of mindfulness:

- Dramatically **improves our stress management**, making us better able to deal with challenges created by work and family stress, deadlines and personal conflict.

- Creates **greater mental clarity and focus**, upgrading our capacity for critical thinking and problem solving.

- Unleashes our capacity for **innovation and creativity** – of benefit both personally and professionally.

- **Enhances our focus on the present moment**, thereby promoting greater engagement in the here and now, enriching our experience of each and every day.

- Improves awareness of our own thought processes and the emotions they trigger, enabling **more effective emotional regulation and resilience**.

- Promotes **new possibilities in difficult personal relationships** both at work and home by replacing habitual reactions with more considered responses.

- Increases our capacity to read other people, to understand where they are coming from, and **enhances empathy**.

- Supports a more panoramic perspective, **better able to manage change**.

- **Deepens our appreciation of the greater meaning and purpose in what we do**.

From '*The Benefits of Mindfulness*' by David Michie.

Ian Gawler, one of Australia's most experienced authorities on mind, body, medicine and meditation, recommends that:

Meditation requires a strong commitment to:

- working on yourself
- breaking old, unhealthy habits of thinking
- dealing with in-built resistance
- regular practice
- patiently persevering through uncomfortable times

Here are some personal motivations that people have nominated to help them to sustain their commitment to meditation:

- to enjoy more peace of mind
- to become a more loving person
- to be less fearful and defensive
- to know their own mind better
- to become a better person
- to stop struggling with self, others and life
- to perform better at work or in sport
- to know oneself more deeply
- to promote health and healing
- to follow a spiritual reawakening or calling
- to lighten up and drop some seriousness
- to release old resentments

Continue your meditation journey as a personal kindness. "Whatever you can do, or dream you can do, begin it … begin it now."

Mindfulness-Based Stillness Meditation (MBSM)

The four steps of MBSM are preparation, relaxation, mindfulness and stillness.

Preparation – is to do with all the practical details of where you meditate, your posture, attitude and how to set yourself up to begin your meditation practice.

Relaxation – we take time to learn how to relax our body and our mind, which becomes clearer, more settled and we become more aware.

Mindfulness – we give our attention to developing mindfulness more fully and more completely, meaning that we simply learn to pay attention to our present moment experience, free of judgement and free of reaction. In doing so, we learn to let go of worrying about the past and being anxious about the future.

Stillness – as we become more mindful, and learn to give our attention more fully to whatever we are doing in the present moment, we notice a fundamental truth. There is activity in our life and there is stillness. We learn to recognise and to rest in that stillness, which is the true essence of meditation and the true essence of the nature of our mind.

Mindfulness meditation helps us to begin to trust and empower our body and our immune system by enabling us to:

- Let go of some of the excessive thinking that creates catastrophising and panic.

- Allow and accept the healthy process of grieving, and to not struggle with our emotions.

- Spend some time connecting with our body by feeling into the body and giving it attention (non-judgemental presence) through Mindfulness of Body sensations.

From '*Meditation – An In-Depth Guide*' - Ian Gawler and Paul Bedson - 2010 - Allen & Unwin.

One of the major benefits of mindfulness for me is that I am less reactive to stressful situations and therefore have a moment to pause and consider my response. When my cat, Gracie, throws up on the carpet, I don't bat an eyelid now! I can clean up all her messes including the kitty litter tray without any angst and just feel grateful for all that she does for me!

Mindful Colouring In

A few years ago, a novel way to become totally present and focussed was first introduced in France. Colouring in books for adults with very complex and creative designs have become very popular. Because the designs are so intricate, it takes a lot of attention and dexterity to accurately fill in the design. They have been used as part of a program of therapy for patients with mental health disorders and I have even seen young people waiting for a delayed plane to take off, colouring in! It is probably quite a successful and enjoyable way to be mindful! Because when you are truly mindful and in the present moment, you are not aware of past and future concerns. Some people find that jigsaw puzzles have the same effect.

Reducing stress, tension and trauma

I have learnt many techniques to reduce my stress and the consequences of past trauma, mostly to help me to sleep. The first of these was Emotional Freedom Technique (EFT) which I learnt from Steve Wells, who is an internationally-acclaimed psychologist and peak performance coach resident in Perth, Western Australia. Steve's research on EFT, in collaboration with Dr David Lake of Sydney, has contributed to the body of knowledge about EFT and its acceptance as an appropriate modality in energy psychology.

This technique, also known as 'Tapping', has multiple applications and information can easily be accessed through Nick Ortner in the USA, who provides education and validation via his website, books and DVDs. Nick organises an online summit every year which is attended by hundreds of thousands of interested people who wish to use the technique in a variety of ways, to reduce anxiety, lose weight, improve relationships, and many other self-improvement strategies. Nick's website is www.thetappingsolution.com

Steve has been a presenter on these summits but one of his major contributions has been devising a simplified version of EFT with his colleague, Dr David Lake, called Simple Energy Techniques (SET). This research on SET demonstrated that by using this simple tapping technique for up to an hour a day, there is a calming effect on the nervous system.

The process of EFT involves tapping with the fingertips on certain meridian points to encourage the flow of energy which may be blocked. These points are based on the meridians explained in Chinese medicine. They include the top of the head, the inside of the eyebrow, the outside of the eyebrow, below the eye, below the nostrils, below the lips on the chin, on the clavicle, and in the armpit. Certain scripts are used during the tapping process to identify problems and feelings which may be positively affected by the tapping. Tapping is a technique usually used as part of a therapy program undertaken by psychologists. However individuals can learn the technique themselves to deal with their problems or what they hope to achieve in life.

The beauty of SET is that no script is required. Feelings can be acknowledged and the tapping technique involves the hands only so it can be used subtly, even in public. I tend to use SET before a challenging appointment such as with a dentist or doctor, or any situation which may cause me a little apprehension. I find SET can also be used to settle oneself for sleep at night. There is plenty of free information and resources on Steve Wells' website www.eftdownunder.com which includes instructions for tapping with diagrams of the points for EFT and SET.

Trauma Release Exercises (TRE)

I was very fortunate to discover Trauma Release Exercises (TRE), which were initially created by Dr David Berceli. I was introduced to TRE thanks to Richmond Heath, a physiotherapist who was also the only

person in Australia trained by Dr Berceli to be a Level 3 Trainer. At the time, I was dealing with a diagnosis of Post-Traumatic Stress Disorder (PTSD) which was affecting my ability to sleep. Many treatment techniques for PTSD require revisiting the trauma whilst in therapy, but I found that I could not tolerate this as the process re-traumatised me. It is not necessary to revisit the trauma with TRE so this is a huge advantage.

Dr Berceli was an American aid worker in the Middle East and was subjected to bombardment. He observed his own reactions and those of the people he was with. He noticed that after the bombing, the children would shake, but the adults didn't. He asked them why and was told that they didn't want the children to know that they were scared.

Dr Berceli became intrigued by the stress response and proceeded to research it thoroughly. He came to the conclusion that the shaking that follows the stress response is the natural resolution of the stress and tension held in the body induced by traumatic incidents. However, shaking is generally perceived as weakness or a psychological problem. This behaviour has been observed in mammals which may fight or flee when threatened, or experience a freeze response. They have been observed to spend some time shaking after these events and then continue on their way. If you have a domestic animal, you may have observed this behaviour as well.

Dr Berceli created a set of exercises to stretch and challenge the leg muscles to the point of fatigue. These are done initially in standing and include standing against the wall with knees at a right angle in a sitting position. This position rapidly fatigues the leg muscles. You then lie on the floor with your knees bent and your feet on the floor. You lift the pelvis and hold it for as long as possible. After lowering the pelvis, by moving the knees towards and away from each other, a tremor develops

which is involuntary and can travel upwards through the body. Termed a neurogenic tremor, it allows the tension and trauma held in the body to dissipate. It is now recognised that stress and trauma are not just psychological problems, but are held in the body.

There are three levels of training. In Level 1, you can learn the technique for yourself. In Level 2, you become skilled in sharing the technique with others, i.e. family and friends. In Level 3, you can train others to do Level 1. TRE was introduced into Australia in 2011 and I was introduced to it by Richmond and subsequently did training with Dr Berceli and experienced a one-to-one session with him. It is a very effective technique and you can find more details on the internet. TRE is now generally recognised as a technique for reducing everyday stress and tension, as well as dealing with PTSD. Dr Berceli has introduced TRE to military personnel returning home from war zones, as well as to people who have experienced natural disasters and conflict.

There are many people who may have experienced PTSD who might benefit from TRE, such as first responders, doctors, nurses, paramedics, police and search and rescue personnel. Often their occupation subjects them to traumatic and challenging situations. In Australia, natural disasters such as floods, bushfires, cyclones and drought often affect whole communities who suffer the consequences.

Hidden wounds

One organisation in Western Australia is raising awareness about PTSD by providing educational seminars in Perth and at several country locations. Partners of Veterans WA Inc. is an organisation established by the partners of veterans of the Vietnam War. Their aim was to support the partners and families of veterans who were known to have many difficulties with their physical and emotional health. Over the years,

the seminars have been made available more widely for anyone at risk of PTSD.

I have had the pleasure of being invited to these seminars to provide the final session. This involves sharing strategies for wellbeing with the audience and introducing them to the benefits of laughter and Laughter Yoga. PTSD is a serious topic, but I refer to it as **P**issed-off and **T**otally **S**tressed-out **D**isorder, which really connects me with the audience and they really need to put a smile on their faces and have a good laugh, as PTSD is not a laughing matter!

Workplace wellbeing

Much of the stress that people experience involves their workplace and travel to and from work. We have already discussed calming strategies which are useful when driving, but self-care at work needs to be a priority. In Japan, unfortunately it is not uncommon for individuals to actually work themselves to death, known as 'karoshi'. This occurs because people work extremely long hours and don't take holidays. The resulting stress causes high blood pressure which contributes to cardiovascular disease and stroke.

What can we learn from this? The ideal occupation involves having your skills and expertise recognised and utilised. You need to have flexibility and autonomy with good teamwork and communication. Achievements need to be recognised and celebrated and there should be opportunities for training and advancement. Changes that occur in the organisation need to be communicated and negotiated, and not just imposed from above. However, much work stress relates to change, which, let's face it, is probably inevitable.

I highly recommend a book by Dr Spencer Johnson called '*Who Moved My Cheese?*' It is a simple parable that reveals profound truths. It involves a delightful story of four characters who live in a maze and look

for cheese to nourish them and make them happy. Cheese is a metaphor for what you want in life – a good job, a loving relationship, money or possessions, health or peace of mind. When the cheese disappears, one of the characters goes searching for new cheese, discovers several truths about change and writes them up on the wall of the maze:

- Change Happens – They keep moving the cheese.

- Anticipate Change – Get ready for the cheese to move.

- Monitor Change – Smell the cheese often so you know when it is getting old.

- Adapt to Change Quickly – The quicker you let go of old cheese, the sooner you can enjoy new cheese.

- Change – Move with the cheese.

- Enjoy Change – Savour the adventure and enjoy the taste of new cheese!

- Be Ready to Change Quickly and Enjoy it Again – They keep moving the cheese.

I find this interpretation of change to be really enlightening! It has been said that it is not the survival of the fittest, but of the most adaptable. These truths about change certainly demonstrate and support this idea.

Research has shown that those with the most autonomy in the workplace are less stressed and healthier. Workplace stress creates health issues, resulting in lost productivity, increased absenteeism, workers' compensation claims and decreased corporate profits due to both physical and emotional illness.

You can outsmart stress with multiple strategies including healthy lifestyle choices, emotional intelligence, resilience, positive attitudes and creative solutions. Try the strategies below to enhance your worklife:

Change

- Commitment – Be involved in ongoing events – don't feel isolated.

- Control – Try to influence the outcome – don't become passive and powerless. Accept what you cannot change.

- Challenge – Change can be positive or negative and can be viewed as an opportunity for new learning. Change is inevitable!

Deadlines

- Plan, prioritise and negotiate prime time without distractions/ interruptions.

- Control phone calls and emails and allocate time and space for the project.

- Collaborate and delegate. Use a 'Do Not Disturb' sign! Request an extension!

Physical and Emotional Wellbeing

- Try postural awareness and regular breaks to breathe, meditate, stretch, and move, whether seated or standing.

- Avoid static postures for long periods and wear comfortable clothing and footwear.

- Drink plenty of water and make healthy nutrition a priority.

- Add enjoyable physical activity to your day.

- Avoid unhealthy habits and negative thinking.

- Avoid unhealthy coping strategies which may provide temporary relief but don't solve the problem.

- Work Smarter, Not Harder. Discover your strengths.

- Acknowledge and appreciate your own and others' achievements and accomplishments.

Communication

- Use emotional intelligence to respond rather than react.

- Recognise and respond appropriately to your own and others' emotions.

- Cultivate calmness.

- Use effective interpersonal communication and utilise appropriate systems and checklists.

- Be prepared to listen, negotiate and double-check.

- Connect with people and develop positive relationships.

- Practice altruism and loving kindness – do a favour every day.

- Play, smile and laugh – be present in the moment.

Laughter Yoga in the workplace

In recent years, Laughter Yoga has been introduced into workplaces and businesses and the outcomes and benefits evaluated at Deakin University in Victoria. Staff who participated in a Laughter Yoga session during their lunchbreak were found to have an improved sense of wellbeing, to be more relaxed and productive during the afternoon, and with an increase in self-advocacy. Laughter Yoga puts everyone on the same level, helps people to connect and is a great way to enhance communication and teamwork, reduce absenteeism and presenteeism (people who are present but not really functioning). There can be an increase in morale and commitment which has a positive benefit on the bottom line. Regular Laughter Yoga sessions can certainly help to reduce work stress.

Laughter Yoga in the health sector

Laughter Yoga is highly recommended as an adjunct to the management of chronic diseases. The health benefits of laughter are relevant to anyone who wishes to strengthen their immune system, reduce the effects of stress and improve their health and wellbeing. Laughter Yoga can also provide benefits to staff and health professionals whose biggest challenge is to maintain their own health and wellbeing while dealing with daily responsibilities, as well as the vicarious stress of their patients and clients. Laughter is one of the most cost effective remedies for stress reduction.

Laughter Yoga in aged care

The benefits of various forms of 'Laughter Therapy' for older people in residential care are well documented. Laughter Yoga can be introduced to residents as part of any friendship or exercise groups to create fun

and laughter and to add quality to life. Staff can also benefit from brief Laughter Yoga sessions to reduce stress, enhance teamwork and improve wellbeing.

Laughter Yoga for mental health

Laughter Yoga is recommended for people experiencing depression and other disorders because of the mood lifting effect of laughter, which is aerobic exercise that releases endorphins. Laughter Clubs reduce isolation and welcome people into a community that supports and includes them, where they can rediscover their laughter and playfulness in a safe environment.

Laughter Yoga for people with disabilities

Many benefits have been experienced by people with disabilities who attend Laughter Yoga with increasing enjoyment. Social and physical skills have improved and Laughter Yoga has become a significant part of their recreation, improving their quality of life. Carers can benefit also, as well as learn Laughter Yoga to incorporate into their groups.

Laughter Yoga in education

Students of all ages from kindergarten to university, as well as teaching staff, can benefit from the introduction of Laughter Yoga into classrooms. Learning is facilitated by a positive environment where students are alert, stress levels are reduced and motivation is increased. Laughter Yoga has the potential to enhance attention and wellbeing in classrooms.

As I have indicated above, there are many different environments and workplaces where staff and clients can improve their wellbeing by participating in Laughter Yoga. Corporate organisations are realising

the value of investing in the health and wellbeing of their staff to improve morale, reduce sick leave and increase staff retention. Investing in training staff to do Laughter Yoga in the workplace is certainly a strategy with potential!

What strategies could you use to improve your wellbeing in the workplace?

_____

_____

If you don't already meditate, how could you initiate learning this skill?

_____

_____

How could you invite more laughter into your life?

_____

_____

> *"To thy known self be true, and it must follow as the night the day, thou canst not then be false to any man."*
> *— William Shakespeare*

Chapter 6

❀

The Art of Wellbeing
- Simple Pleasures

Chapter 6

The Art of Wellbeing - Simple Pleasures

> *"They should remember their pleasures with gratitude, as they would the harvest of a summer."* — Kahlil Gibran

Pleasure can provide us with a range of positive emotions such as enjoyment, delight, laughter, satisfaction, excitement, wonder and so on. Pleasures which are shared enhance the experience! You can reduce the effects of stress, create more balance and improve your wellbeing by adding simple pleasures to your daily life.

Add your own favourites to this list and incorporate at least six of them into your life each day. Do this particularly when you are experiencing your early warning signs of stress and wish to improve how you feel. Remember that you can reinforce the positive pathways in your brain by **'Taking in the Good'**, savouring all the small, beautiful, joyful, amusing and endearing moments in your day. Use your senses to outsmart stress!

I am giving you some examples in each category and then you can fill in your own choices.

LOOK	What do you love to look at that gives you pleasure and enjoyment?
	Beauty/Colour/
	Sunset _____
LISTEN	What sounds do you enjoy and that bring back positive memories?
	Favourite Music/
	Birdsong _____

SMELL	What aromas and scents do you enjoy? Lavender/Coffee	_____
TASTE	What are your favourite healthy foods? Thai Food/Mango	_____
FEEL	What are the many ways you can enjoy pleasurable sensations through the skin? Hug/Massage/Bath	_____
MOVE	Enjoyable movement is crucial for our health. What moves do you make? Dance/Yoga/ Feldenkrais	_____
NATURE	There is so much nature to enjoy – what are your favourites? Sky/Ocean/Trees/ Pets	_____
PEOPLE	Who are the people who nurture you and care about your wellbeing? Family/Friends	_____
PLACES	Do you have memories of special holidays or favourite locations? Holiday Places/ Gardens	_____
CREATE	What creative pursuits have you had in the past or enjoy now? Art/Writing/Music	_____
FUN	What do you like to do just for fun? Outings/Picnic/Films	_____
LAUGH	Who are the people that you share the most laughter with? Family/Friends	_____

SELF-TALK	What kind and caring words can you say to yourself?	
	I am Kind/Generous	_____
REWARD	Acknowledge what you have done well and reward yourself!	
	Retail Therapy/ Massage	_____
SOLITUDE	How can you find enough quiet times to reflect and relax?	
	Quiet Times/ Meditation	_____
GRATITUDE	Have you found three things to be grateful for today?	
	Health/Love/Support	_____
ATTITUDE	Recognise all your positive attributes and attitudes.	
	Kind/Empathic/ Flexible	_____

With all this emphasis on using pleasure to enhance your wellbeing, I am not advocating being selfish, self-indulgent or narcissistic! We just need healthy pleasures in our lives to improve how we feel. By noticing all the potentially pleasurable moments in our lives, we are being mindful and we have much to be grateful for. All these moments can be experienced and savoured in order to **'Take in the Good',** as recommended by Dr Rick Hanson.

Some of my favourite pleasures include my morning muesli and real coffee and chopping a variety of vegetables for soup or salad (mindfulness is essential for this latter task in order to preserve one's fingers!) Classical music is my constant companion and other sounds that delight me include the laughter of children, early morning birdsong and rain on a tin roof. Skype provides me with the images and voices of close family and friends, and photos and videos of my brand new grandson often arrive via the internet. The closeness that this creates is very precious.

My favourite tactile pleasures (which includes sensations felt through the skin) include a hot shower, hugs, massage and stroking my cat, Gracie.

Hugs

Hugs are an important aspect of human communication. They are easy to share and democratic, so that anyone can benefit from them and hugging does no harm to the environment! There are many types of hugs such as the A-frame hug, heart-to-heart hug, side-by-side hug and the front-to-back hug, which is a useful hug to give to someone who is doing the washing up for you! It is important however to ask permission before sharing a hug. Hugs are useful as a greeting with family and friends, but they also are part of celebrations and commiserations, and can be more eloquent than words. We all need 'hug-friends' to make the most of our life journey.

Over the years, I have exchanged hugs over the phone, to end a conversation. These were silent hugs to start with but one day my son was feeling very exuberant and contributed sound effects as if he was hugging me really strongly! I fell about laughing and joined in! So I think of a silent hug as a virtual hug and a hug with sound effects as an audible hug! If you end a conversation with someone who you care about, who is far away, then this type of hug will make a positive ending as you say good bye. Try it and see!

I have already given you some of my favourite pleasures in the list above, so enjoy filling in your own list.

Why not start your own Wellbeing Revolution!

Nature – the seasons

The beauty of nature and of the seasons has been fully expressed in the paintings of Vincent van Gogh. I was given a book of his paintings for my 21st birthday many years ago and one particular painting was my favourite. Called Evening Walk, it depicted a scene at sunset with an orange horizon, dark blue hills and an olive grove. In the foreground, a man and a woman are taking a walk. By chance, I found a print of this picture, the original of which is held in a private collection, but I have never seen it in any other book or exhibition. This picture has been hanging on my wall ever since!

The value of spending time in nature is being recommended more and more for its benefits. In Japan, since 1988, 'forest bathing' has been recommended as a significant health activity. People are encouraged to enjoy the beauties of nature. Cherry blossom time in the spring is a prime example, but there are also many gardens, ancient temples and wild forest terrains which people can access and enjoy. This is known as 'Shinrin-yoku' forest therapy, the medicine of simply being in the forest or taking in the forest atmosphere. It has become a cornerstone of preventive health care and healing in Japanese medicine.

Researchers are amassing a body of evidence, proving what we all know to be true. Nature is good for us and has both long and short term mental and physical health benefits. So many people in large, busy cities lack access to the benefits of nature and this has been described as 'Nature Deficiency Disorder'.

There is something innate about our connection to nature. In a study published in the *'American Journal of Alzheimer's Disease & Other Dementias'*, patients with dementia and Alzheimer's are known to have decreased symptoms following time in gardens or being exposed to horticultural therapy.

There is so much to nature – the sky, clouds, rainbows and birds, parks, trees, gardens, flowers, butterflies and of course, fruit and vegetables. Gardeners are said to be happier because of their sense of purpose, physical activity and the enjoyment of the fruit of their labours. City dwellers can benefit from pots on their balconies, as well as communal gardens, which connect people and result in social benefits. Pets are, of course, part of the nature that we enjoy, as well as domestic and wild animals.

In his documentaries, the inspirational Sir David Attenborough has shared so many wonders of the natural world, which we can enjoy as well. From the tiniest insects to the largest whale, he has shared the beauty, uniqueness, idiosyncrasies and habitats of most of the creatures on the planet. This surely reminds us of the amazing diversity and beauty of nature and inspires us to explore it for ourselves.

A large percentage of our planet is water so the ocean, rivers and lakes provide us with many water-based activities for our enjoyment. It is to be hoped that we can preserve the pristine environment which still exists in parts of the world. Our forests are the lungs of the planet!

Of course, how we spend time in nature depends very much on where we live and the current season. Summer and winter have different appeal at different times, depending on which hemisphere you inhabit. Spring and autumn bring their own delights.

Here in Australia, summer can be very hot and intense and last summer, I was invited to write a blog for the Playgroup WA website and Facebook page which I would like to share with you. You may find it helpful, especially if you have kids in your life!

Ten Cool Tips for a Long Hot Summer

1. **Keep cool** – there are many ways to keep you all cool before you switch on the aircon! Lots of cool water to drink, a squirty bottle is great fun, cool cotton clothes, a wet hand towel wrapped around your neck, a fan and damp clothes have a great effect. All water play is supervised, of course, and CPR training is a must! If you arrive home on a really hot day, try having a cold shower to cool down and imagine you are standing under a waterfall. Your brain doesn't know it's not a real waterfall!

2. **Keep calm** – summer heat leads to frazzlement for kids and parents, so try taking slow breaths to calm yourself, and remain focussed and consistent as you meet your kids' needs. Meditation helps too.

3. **Gratitude** – many positive emotions contribute to our wellbeing. Gratitude helps you to recognise all the small, beautiful, joyful, funny, endearing and delicious moments in your day. Write three of them down every night in your gratitude journal and also focus on love, appreciation, kindness and optimism.

4. **Play** – the most precious time you can spend with your kids is when you all play together. Make play a priority at home, in parks, at the beach and wherever you are on holidays. Fun and laughter shared together will enhance your holiday time. Lots of physical fun helps kids to sleep better too. Adults who play will enhance their wellbeing and Laughter Yoga is the easiest way to rediscover your playfulness.

5. **Connect** – positive relationships develop when we socialise and share time with family and friends. Make the most of your connections, share what you enjoy together whether it is at home or out in the community. Make parent play dates, as well as kids' play dates!!

6. **Relax** – hot weather is tiring, so imagine you live in the Mediterranean and schedule a siesta for the family. JelliTime™ is a game in which you can play, learn, laugh and relax with the kids. JelliTime can be a fun, engaging and nurturing activity which the whole family can share and enjoy together.

7. **Mindful eating** – we are blessed with a vast array of healthy fruit and veg, a whole rainbow, in fact. Mindful shopping, food preparation, cooking and eating can become a multi-sensory pleasure as you focus on the shape, colour, texture, aroma and crunch of your meals. Share as many meals as possible around your table and try discussing all the good things for which you are grateful.

8. **Limit technology** – if you increase your playtime, book reading and games times with your kids so they are having more fun, you may find that screen time loses some fascination. Maybe just allow screen time as a reward or when you really need to focus on something else.

9. **Give** – when you give, you also receive – so share affection, hugs, massage, child-minding, play, fun, laughter, chores and of course, healthy food, gratitude and appreciation.

10. **Celebrate** – every family develops its own rituals and celebrations for birthdays, Christmas and other holidays. For a reverse Advent Calendar, it is suggested you place an item of food in a basket on each of the twelve days of Christmas and then donate it. Celebrate all the achievements and accomplishments of your family and anticipate the next year with optimism.

Those of you in the Northern Hemisphere are probably well-practiced in peacefully co-existing with very cold and icy weather. Here in Australia, although we don't experience such low temperatures, winter weather

can increase the risk of health issues for older people. So here are a few ways you can stay winter-wise when the cold weather hits.

Ten Warm Tips for a Long Cold Winter

1. Wear layers of clothing that you can adjust according to the indoor or outdoor temperature.

2. Add boots, gloves and scarves, jacket and coats if you are venturing outside.

3. Indoors, I add long socks and ugg boots and find that a hot water bottle clasped to my middle while I am watching television is very cosy. Also, I am fortunate that my cat, Gracie, likes to sit on my lap and provide another source of heat!

4. Winter is the season of delicious soups and casseroles, and if you make a large quantity, you can freeze several serves to make life easier.

5. In summer, Australians will often go to the movies or the local shopping centre to enjoy the air-conditioning. So I suppose you could do the same thing in the winter to keep warm!

6. If you are cold when you get home, enjoy a nice hot shower or bath, put on warm clothes and enjoy a hot drink.

7. In my skiing days, I was introduced to mulled wine, also known as gluwein, which is a delicious concoction of red wine, spices such as cinnamon, nutmeg and cloves, and some citrus slices. You can add a little water and sugar to taste and gently heat. The alcohol (theoretically) evaporates with the heat and this drink

will certainly warm you up! Skiing is one of the pleasures of winter time!

8. Enjoyable physical activity will warm you up as well. Walking in the great outdoors when the sun is out would be a pleasure. Be wary of wet, slippery or icy surfaces. Indoor activities such as dancing, table tennis or any other form of exercise will stimulate your circulation and generate some warmth.

9. Attend a Laughter Club and participate in Laughter Yoga. It is lots of fun, and as it is aerobic exercise, you will definitely get warmer!

10. As a last resort, use some form of heating at home for a short period of time to raise the indoor temperature. A cosy fire and hot chocolate are a good combination!

Of course, we mustn't forget the beauties and joys of autumn and spring. Perhaps I will allow you to explore and decide for yourself your favourite moments to savour during these seasons! Perhaps you have some favourite memories of these seasons which you can remember and enjoy again! Make the most of every season!

Hygge

In Denmark, which is considered to be one of the happiest countries on the planet, the Danes have a tradition called 'Hygge' (pronounced Hooga) which means 'cosiness'. The word comes from a Norwegian word meaning 'wellbeing'.

In essence, hygge means creating a warm atmosphere and enjoying the good things in life with good people. The warm glow of candlelight is

hygge. Friends and family – that's hygge too. There's nothing more hygge than sitting round a table, discussing the big and small things in life. It can be anything that makes life more enjoyable, such as having a coffee while waiting at the laundromat. Perhaps hygge explains why the Danes are some of the happiest people in the world?

To me, hygge is about positive emotions and positive relationships, finding pleasure and self-nurture in everyday life and sharing it. In fact, you can find it anywhere!

What are your favourite summer pleasures?

_____

_____

What do you enjoy most about winter?

_____

_____

What can you add to your life that is Hygge?

_____

_____

"If you truly love nature, you will find beauty everywhere."
— Vincent van Gogh

Chapter 7

❀

Love, Respect and Nurture Your Body, Mind and Spirit

Chapter 7
Love, Respect and Nurture Your Body,
Mind and Spirit

"To keep the body in good health is a duty ... otherwise we shall not be able to keep our mind strong and clear." — Buddha

So much information is available from multiple sources about how we should optimise our health. Over time, much of it is contradictory, so accessing reputable sources is important.

The choices we do make need to be motivated by our attitude to ourselves. Love and respect, and being our own best friend, will help us make the healthy choices that will provide the optimal environment for us to thrive. I will try to simplify the information for you that I feel is relevant. I have developed a To Do List to help you make those healthy choices.

HEALTHY CHOICES – MY TO DO LIST

OUTSMART STRESS	Notice your early signs of STRESS and do something about it! Choose a healthy coping strategy as outlined in Chapters 4 and 5.
BREATHE	Use your BREATH to reduce tension and calm yourself. Oxygen is an essential ingredient required by all our cells, so that they can all function optimally in whatever system or organ they exist. Breathing efficiently is critical. Have you noticed how your brain regulates your breathing depending on your activity? If you

run for a bus, you will be feeling breathless by the time you reach your seat as you compensate for the additional oxygen requirements.

SMILE   Even if you don't feel like it, put a SMILE on your face and receive a dose of endorphins. You will feel better! Make the most of your mirror neurons!

LAUGH   Use your LAUGHTER PRESCRIPTION to benefit from more laughter in your life.

> *"Laughter is the shortest distance between two people."*
> *- Victor Borge*

SUNLIGHT   Regular safe exposure to sunlight by which Vitamin D is absorbed by the skin is an important contribution to health. Many people are deficient in Vitamin D as they try to avoid sunburn by protecting their skin, staying indoors and not receiving sufficient exposure. Sunlight also stimulates the production of the hormone melatonin which contributes to our ability to fall asleep at the end of the day.

MOVE & ENJOY   BE ACTIVE every day for the physical and emotional benefits. We will discuss this further in Chapter 10.

REAL FOOD   Choose FOOD as close to its natural state as possible for maximum nutritional benefits. Avoid processed foods. The MEDITERRANEAN DIET has all the necessary ingredients for health

and wellbeing. Sharing a meal and socialising enhances the benefits! I discuss food as fuel in more detail below.

H₂O

Drink enough WATER regularly, so every cell in your body can function properly. The body is 70% water so replacing lost water is a priority. Dehydration can cause headaches and with vigorous physical activity or hot weather, replacement is crucial. 6-8 glasses daily are recommended.

↓ CHEMICALS

Reduce your intake of CHEMICALS in food, drinks, personal and household products including LEGAL, PRESCRIPTION and ILLEGAL DRUGS. To the body, chemicals are foreign material that can be toxic and have significant adverse effects.

↑ AFDs

It is recommended to have three or four ALCOHOL FREE DAYS per week to preserve your brain and liver.

MASSAGE

Having a massage is a great way to relax and reduce the effects of stress. Try giving and receiving a SHOULDER MASSAGE and BACK SCRATCH to share the benefits, or book a massage with a therapist.

SLEEP

Good sleep is an essential part of a healthy life and requires regular hours in a darkened room. Take a nap during the day to give yourself a nurture break and reduce stress. More information about optimal conditions for sleep are in Chapter 11.

RELAXATION   You can elicit the Relaxation Response (the opposite to the fight or flight response) by using breathing exercises, guided imagery, progressive muscle relaxation, meditation and yoga, as well as EFT and SET which we have already discussed. The Relaxation Response was identified by Dr Herbert Benson and it is important to know that it can be easily accessed to reduce the effects of stress.

MINDFULNESS   Use all your senses to give full attention to what you are doing in the present moment. See Chapter 5 for more information.

NURTURE   Fill in the list of SIMPLE PLEASURES and add them to your day to enhance your WELLBEING and reduce the effects of STRESS.

CONNECTION   We have already discussed the importance of positive emotions and relationships which give us a sense of belonging and contribute to our wellbeing. Our relationship with ourselves is important and is reflected in the quality of our interactions with others.

Fuel for the body

Food is such an important and essential ingredient for life. The choice of foods that we have is amazing! So what guides us to choose the most appropriate foods for health? In our busy lives, convenience foods beckon, but they are often very different from the basic diets that our grandparents relied on. It is said that if your grandmother wouldn't recognise it, don't eat it. The term 'Frankenfood' has been created to describe heavily processed foods laced with preservatives, additives, unhealthy fats, artificial colours and sweeteners, as well as chemicals

for flavour and increased shelf life. So take time when you are shopping to read all the labels and avoid all these ingredients. You also need to look out for unhealthy fats and added sugar which has many names such as those ending in 'ose' and includes honey and agave! Many so-called healthy low-fat foods are loaded with sugar, such as breakfast cereals and muesli bars. Artificial sweeteners have been found to add weight, and aspartame in particular is considered to be neurotoxic and has been banned in Europe.

What is recommended is REAL FOOD which is plant-based and preferably grown in optimal conditions with minimal pesticides and other chemicals. Lean protein from grass-fed free range animals is preferred, as animals raised in concentrated animal-feeding operations (CAFOs) are not considered to be very healthy. Wild caught fish, such as salmon, is preferable to those which are farmed and contaminated. The larger the fish, the more likely it is to have mercury present due to the pollution of the waterways. Eggs from free range poultry are preferred to what is known as 'cage eggs'.

Eating seasonal, locally produced fruit and vegetables means that they are fresher, and if you have access to a farmer's market, you will do even better! Much produce is shipped around the world which contributes to a carbon footprint, and freshness and freedom from pesticides is not a guarantee.

Sugar and flour

It is being recognised that an excessive intake of sugar and products containing sugar has a very negative effect on health, contributes to obesity and multiple chronic diseases. Flour, being a simple carbohydrate, also contributes to this situation. There is a huge amount of information on the internet about healthy eating versus dieting. Susan Peirce Thompson PhD has developed a system of healthy eating called *'Bright Line Eating'* to assist people to overcome food addictions,

which she herself experienced. She specialises in understanding food addictions and recommends removing sugar and flour (gluten) from the diet, having three meals only a day, no snacks, weighing portions and writing every evening the planned meals for the following day. This establishes new eating habits and helps to overcome the need for comfort foods which are often carbohydrates. The resulting weight loss can be maintained by continuing this approach to nutrition. Susan's book *'Bright Line Eating'* was published in 2017.

Another interesting book, *'Outsmart Sugar'* by Tara C. Mitchell, shows how easy it is to outsmart sugar using simple, effective techniques that really work. Tara shares, in a very entertaining way, a step-by-step plan to reprogram your subconscious reaction to sugar, deactivate your cravings and give you back full control. Tara is also a reformed sugar addict!

The Mediterranean Diet

Much has been written about the Mediterranean Diet, which consists of lean protein, fruit, vegetables, legumes, nuts, red wine and olive oil. Each of these components has been well-researched for the individual nutritional benefits they contribute. However, I believe that it is the communal sharing of meals involving several generations that also contributes to the success of this approach to nutrition. The preparation, serving and sharing of delicious, healthy food accompanied by good wine, conversation, laughter and a sense of belonging is way superior to eating fast food on your own!

Weight control

Having a healthy weight is a challenge for many of us. It is now recognised that diets per se may contribute to weight loss in the short term, however weight is often regained afterwards. Some time ago, I found an interesting list of 24 ways to lose weight without dieting. This

has now been updated on the internet, illustrated by slide shows, but there were some key recommendations which I found useful and would like to share with you.

- Eat more slowly, and savour each bite so that the body has time to trigger fullness hormones. It takes the brain 20 minutes to register that you have had enough!

- Use smaller dishes for portion control. In my boarding school days, we had to eat everything on the plate regardless of whether we liked it or had had enough. This habit was very hard to eradicate, but smaller portions really help.

- During a meal, you will notice a pause in your eating. This is the time to stop eating rather than continue until you are really full.

- Use the 80/20 rule. In Okinawa, there is a term called 'hara hachi bu' which means eat until 80% full, which ties in with the previous point. You could also serve 20% less food, which fits in with portion control on smaller dishes.

- Cut back on sugar, particularly in soft drinks/sodas and fruit juice.

- Eat more vegetarian meals, which include fibre, vitamins and antioxidants in fruit and vegetables.

- Eat more home-cooked meals, then you truly have control over creating healthy nutrition.

- Drink plenty of water, green tea and reduce your alcohol intake.

- Sleep more. Sleep deprived individuals tend to put on weight.

- Regular exercise can be achieved with a daily walk, housework, gardening, as well as choosing games, sports, dancing and laughing!

Mindful eating

We have already discussed mindfulness but there are a few additional ways to really appreciate preparing and eating your food. Consider the origin of your food and all the people who grew it, harvested it and transported it. It grew thanks to nature - the soil, sun, rain and wind.

Cook with love, whether you are eating alone or sharing with others. Try a variety of ethnic foods from different regions of the world and be adventurous. Eat familiar food with curiosity and really notice the flavours and textures.

Buy local produce whenever possible; it will be fresher and have a smaller carbon footprint. I love asparagus but not if it has travelled a long distance across the globe! Buy meat from animals that have been treated respectfully.

Really notice the aroma of food before you eat it. Does it bring up any memories? It is best to just focus on eating. Sometimes we read or watch television which diminishes our ability to fully enjoy the food.

If you live alone, still go to the trouble of preparing healthy food and making it look attractive on the plate. This is really a sign of being your own best friend and treating yourself with love and respect.

Invite a friend or friends over to share a meal with you, which really improves your enjoyment!

We are blessed with a huge variety of healthy foods to choose from, for which I am extremely grateful.

Nutrition

In a recent article on Medscape, it was suggested that as nutrition is a critical component to human health, doctors could share the following six evidence-based tips with their patients.

1.   Choose foods with a wide variety of colours and textures in their most natural forms.

2.   Avoid or dramatically minimise processed foods.

3.   Choose realistic balanced diets for weight loss and weight maintenance. Dieters fail on diets that are too restrictive, unbalanced or cause rapid weight loss.

4.   Consume healthy oils for heart health such as fish, olives and avocado.

5.   Forego red meat and live longer, substituting fish, poultry, legumes, nuts and wholegrains.

6.   Consume fermented foods/probiotics and fibre for gastrointestinal and overall health.

Optimal foods

Research has demonstrated that many foods are rich in vitamins, minerals and antioxidants. The good news is that both dark chocolate and red wine contain antioxidants, so to have them in moderation without guilt is possible! Milk chocolate and white chocolate are not recommended.

Green vegetables – there is such a huge variety to choose from; some you can eat fresh and raw, others can be steamed, stir-fried, baked or

included in soups. They include kale, spinach, lettuce, arugula (also known as rocket), artichokes, broccoli, asparagus, celery, leeks, zucchini, brussel sprouts, bok choy, bell peppers, cabbage, cucumber, green beans, peas, sprouts and many more. A recent gadget called a spiralizer will allow you to turn zucchini and carrots into 'vegetable spaghetti' which provides a healthy basis for a salad or as a substitute for pasta!

In addition, there are many other colourful vegetables which provide a rainbow of choice. Some examples include tomatoes, carrots, squash, eggplant, capsicum, chillies, sweet potatoes, mushrooms, avocados, onions, radishes, pumpkin. Several serves a day are recommended.

Protein should be added to every meal and there are many sources to choose from such as eggs, chicken or turkey, cottage cheese, milk, Greek yoghurt, lean beef, fresh fish or seafood, canned tuna or salmon. You can also snack on almonds or cheese, and nuts and vegetables also have protein content.

Healthy fats are now considered to be a significant part of a healthy diet. Those found in oily fish, olives, olive oil, coconut oil, walnut oil, sesame oil and flaxseed oil are considered beneficial, as well as avocados. It is important to avoid heavily processed vegetable oils such as canola and safflower. Trans-fats are now being banned from processed foods around the world and a small amount of butter is healthier for you than processed margarine.

Fruit is an important part of good nutrition, preferably eaten whole to receive the full benefit of the fibre which slows down the absorption of the sugar content. Apparently, if you blitz fruit in a smoothie, the sugar content is absorbed more rapidly. Fruit juice delivers a significant dose of sugar without the fibre and it is best to avoid it. Red grapes provide resveratrol even before they become red wine! Again, we have a whole rainbow of fruit to enjoy, so adding two serves a day will do you some good!

Berries, especially blueberries, are recommended for their strong antioxidant and anti-inflammatory properties.

Nuts and seeds are recommended as one of the healthiest snacks, preferably with minimal processing and nothing else added. Research shows that people who eat nuts reduce the risk factors for chronic diseases, including heart disease and diabetes. They live longer than those who do not. Nuts contain healthy fats, fibre and protein, and you can take your pick from almonds, walnuts, cashews, hazelnuts, brazil nuts, macadamias and pecans. Peanuts, also known as ground nuts, are actually a legume, and are often heavily salted. Nutritious seeds include pepitas, sunflower seeds, flaxseeds, chia and sesame seeds.

Legumes, also known as pulses, provide a wide variety of nutrients and are a healthy and economic food everyone can include in a balanced diet. They are a good source of fibre and protein, as well as vitamins and minerals, and have a low GI. Examples include split peas, as well as a wide variety of beans, chick peas and lentils. Baked beans are quick and easy, hummus (made from chick peas) is very popular, as well as chilli con carne with added kidney beans. Legumes can easily be added to salads, soups and casseroles.

Fish is considered to be the number one brain food, particularly cold water fish such as tuna, mackerel, herring, anchovies, sardines and wild salmon. However, mercury is a contaminant that needs to be avoided. It is recommended that we should have two to three meals of fish per week as it is full of omega 3 fatty acids. Research suggests that a diet sufficient in omega 3's is vital to help maintain memory and cognition in older people.

Wholegrains are preferred in a diet to refined grains which contribute to an increase in cardiovascular disease and diabetes. They include brown rice, whole oats, whole rye, wholegrain barley (not pearled), buckwheat

(great for pancakes) and quinoa, which is a seed rather than a grain. Quinoa is a great alternative to pasta and white rice. Wholegrain wheat, as well as refined wheat flour, should be avoided if you need to be gluten-free. It is important to read the labels.

Dairy is an important source of calcium but there seems to be some controversy over the value of low-fat versus regular products. Many low-fat products have added sugar or artificial sweeteners which do not contribute to good health. Natural greek yoghurt, which has no additives, is very versatile as it can be used with savoury food or as the basis for a dessert. It contains probiotics which are good for gut health.

Herbs and spices, whether they are fresh or dried, can add colour and flavour to many meals. Turmeric, ginger, cinnamon and black pepper have nutritional value and many leafy herbs can be added to salads or cooking. These include parsley, mint, rosemary, basil, tarragon, oregano, marjoram, chives, coriander, dill, and these can be used to enhance flavour instead of adding salt. Many herbs are infused to create teas, the most well-known being mint, chamomile, lemon and ginger, and of course chai, a spicy tea originating in India. Green tea is thought to have significant health benefits as well.

Family meals are a great opportunity to share your delicious, nutritious food around a table, rather than in front of the television! Some families like to say grace, or at least acknowledge the person who prepared the meal. Children learn table manners and to be included in discussions and news-sharing. One positive practice is for each family member to mention something that they are grateful for that occurred during the day, or a challenge that they faced, or what they are looking forward to tomorrow. Teenagers who adopt an attitude of gratitude benefit from this practice.

If you have been at work all day and still have to prepare the evening meal, would it be a good idea to sit down and watch half an hour of

comedy or a quiz show with the family? You can share a good laugh, revitalise yourself and make the evening duties more enjoyable.

What healthy foods do you already enjoy?

_____

_____

What foods could you remove from your diet to improve your health?

_____

_____

What other items on the healthy choice list could you add to your life?

_____

_____

"Life is like riding a bike. You only fall off if you stop peddling. Keep peddling!" — Anon

Chapter 8

❀

Treasure Your Brain

Chapter 8
Treasure Your Brain

> *"Intelligence is the ability to adapt to change."*
> *— Stephen Hawking*

Although research has revealed many of the mysteries of the human brain, it continues to amaze and challenge us. One important aspect of its function is neuroplasticity, which enables the brain to change and adapt, creating new neurons and connections in response to new experiences and learning. If nerve cells are damaged, new cells can be recruited to take over lost function.

Have you ever spent time pondering on all the functions that your brain provides during your lifetime? Although the brain is only 2% of your body weight, it consumes 20% to 25% of your energy. It was originally thought that the adult brain was like a machine and not capable of change or an increase of neurons and connections. Although medical science has discovered many aspects of brain function with increasingly sophisticated research, the following aspects are still not fully understood and continue to be a mystery:

- **Consciousness:** This includes your thoughts, emotions and awareness of your surroundings, also your beliefs, attitudes and values. We need to choose what we think about at times so that we do not focus on past negative events and experiences, and reinforce these pathways in the brain. We need to be more aware of **'Taking in the Good'**.

- **Personality:** Maybe you are born with it or it is influenced by your environment. You may be an introvert or an extrovert but your personality can certainly be altered by trauma, brain surgery or neurological disorders.

- **Memories:** The ability to create, store and retrieve memories continues to be a mystery, especially your ability to recall memory at will. It is known that your memories are not fixed, but can be weakened or strengthened by later events, particularly emotional experiences. There are many activities and systems that you can use to enhance your memory.

- **Intelligence:** This is the ability to learn from experience and relies on your neurons to solve problems and develop learning styles. According to Daniel Goleman, the IQ has its limitations and we can also develop emotional intelligence and social intelligence, which enhance our relationships.

- **Sleep and dreams:** The activities of the brain during sleep and the purpose of dreaming are still not well understood. Proper sleep allows for efficient waste removal, for the brain to rest, and neurons to repair and generate so that we can function better when we wake.

- **Stress:** Research has demonstrated that stress is associated with neural degeneration. Long-term stressful life experiences cause elevated cortisol production, which results in damage to brain cells and inhibits the brain's ability to form new connections between existing cells. This affects the hippocampus, which is one of the few regions of the brain capable of producing new neurons. Shrinking of the hippocampus affects memory.

I think that perhaps there is a parallel situation with our knowledge and use of computers. They are such an integral part of our lives now, for communication, shopping, banking, manufacturing and organising and monitoring multiple aspects of our lives. I can access my emails, social media, webinars, news and information about any topic under the sun, but I have no idea how this is all possible in this digital world! Likewise, even if I do not understand the intricate and mysterious workings of the brain, I can utilise its many functions to my advantage. I understand that thanks to neuroplasticity, my memory, thoughts, ideas, beliefs, perceptions and attitudes and emotions are all adaptable and changeable. I can therefore make a choice about them.

Protection

Protecting the brain from trauma and harm is paramount. Wearing a seatbelt when driving or a helmet when cycling or riding a motorbike is critical to avoiding head injury. There is currently much concern about repeated concussion which many players involved in contact sports can experience. Many types of football and rugby, as well as boxing, place players at risk and even junior teams need to be aware of these risks. Players need to be properly assessed after any knock to the head and should be removed from play if they are experiencing symptoms.

Trauma to the head from a 'one hit coward punch' causes injury at the point of contact, and the impact causes the brain to collide with the skull on the opposite side of the head, creating a 'contra-coup' injury. If the victim falls backwards, causing further damage to the skull and brain, this type of injury is eventually sometimes fatal. There is a huge need to educate young people about the effects of the fight or flight response and how in this state cognitive abilities

in the cortex are repressed. Survival behaviour is a spontaneous reaction expressed in anger and aggression, and moderated by the primitive reptilian brain.

Lifestyle factors

Creating an optimal environment for the brain to function is influenced by our chosen lifestyle. It has been said that what is good for the heart, is good for the brain. Thus, many of the items on the previous healthy choice list would benefit brain health. Having a healthy weight, normal blood pressure, cholesterol, triglyceride and blood glucose levels will benefit your brain. Avoiding chemicals and toxins which are found in air, water, foods, personal and household products will also be beneficial. Other chemicals such as nicotine, alcohol, legal and illegal drugs will also influence brain function.

There are many chronic diseases and neurological conditions which can impact the way your brain behaves. It is now understood that diabetes and depression can lead to dementia. The impact of a stroke on the total function of the individual can be catastrophic. However, because of neuroplasticity, there is potential for regaining function in the long term.

Use it or lose it

Many of the skills that we learn in life become automatic, such as cleaning our teeth or driving a car. These pathways are well-defined, but if we wish to create new pathways, the brain needs new experiences and learning. Repetition is necessary for learning and also speaking and writing information reinforces acquiring new memories. There has been much emphasis on the value of

doing crosswords, Sudoku, and other mind puzzles, however it has been demonstrated that you may improve your skills in these pursuits, but the skills do not generalise. Any new learning builds up cognitive reserve so lifelong learning pays off!

Activities worth pursuing include learning a new language or a musical instrument, taking up a new hobby, utilising the internet or even rediscovering an old interest. In the last few years, I have been trying to learn Japanese and find that it needs regular repetition in order to retain such unfamiliar words. Whenever I buy sushi or see someone with a name tag which looks Japanese, I ask them if they are Japanese and have a short polite conversation with them if they are! I always get a wonderful smiling response if the person IS Japanese!

Another aspect of brain function which needs to be well-used is the sense of humour! Having a robust sense of humour contributes to resilience and our ability to bounce back from the challenges that life presents us! I have found that as I get older, I have more opportunities to laugh at myself. In fact, people of all ages have memory lapses or can't find their keys, glasses or phone! This has been known as a 'senior moment' but current terminology calls this an 'intellectual interlude', which sounds much better!

Multi-tasking

There is a lot of discussion around 'multi-tasking' and women are said to be very competent at this. However, focussing on one thing at a time is said to be more efficient. Divided attention or dual-tasking, where the individual is carrying out more than one task at a time, reduces effectiveness and is sometimes dangerous. This is why texting while driving is illegal because attention is taken

away from the driving task, which is in fact very complex. When driving, we need to be aware of road and weather conditions, our speed, other drivers, traffic lights, pedestrians, the distance between cars, changes in speed and the dangerous tactics of other drivers. Road rules and speed limits need attention as well. All of this should have our full attention and require us to be truly mindful when in charge of a vehicle of any kind. As I often drive alone, I do notice how distracting having a passenger can be and sometimes when we are chatting my car goes on automatic pilot and I miss the turn-off!

Neuroplasticity

Dr Norman Doidge is a psychiatrist and researcher who has explored the concept of neuroplasticity in a documentary and a book, '*The Brain That Changes Itself*'. Providing multiple examples, he demonstrates the ability of the brain to build new networks to compensate for damage and trauma to the brain. In his subsequent book, '*The Brain's Way of Healing*', he further discusses the phenomenon of neuroplasticity, which is considered to be the most important development of our understanding of the brain and mind since the beginning of modern science. Neuroplasticity is the property of the brain that enables it to change its own structure and functioning in response to activity and mental experience. Dr Doidge shares the stories of many people whose neurological problems have been diminished based on this concept. He also shares how to lower our risk of dementia by 60%.

Risk factors for dementia

Many studies have been conducted to identify the risk factors for cognitive decline and dementia, including Alzheimer's, and which lifestyle factors reduce this risk.

Risk factors include old age, family history, Down Syndrome, particular genes, being female, past history of head injury, high blood pressure, high BMI and being a smoker. Having diabetes or depression, Parkinson's Disease or cardiovascular disease may all contribute to the onset of dementia.

Reducing the risk

However, there are several ways to reduce the risk:

- Exercise is the most powerful contributor to decreasing the risk of cognitive decline and dementia. Exercise improves memory and increases the size of the hippocampus. We will discuss this further in Chapter 10.

- Cognitive reserve has also been shown to delay mild cognitive decline, which means the more education you have, the better. Lifelong learning is recommended!

- Healthy diet, which includes three to four servings of fruit and vegetables a day. Food sensitivities, glucose, insulin and obesity affect our brain health.

- Normal weight, with a BMI preferably between 18 and 25.

- Low alcohol intake.

- No smoking.

- Manage your stress, be social and have a laugh.

- Choose positive emotions and positive relationships.

- Use mindfulness and meditation to improve memory.

We did not evolve to sit all day, travel in cars, eat processed food, inhale smoke or drink too much! There is currently much information available about appropriate nutrients for brain health. Obviously, the brain requires an optimal supply of oxygen and water, and uses glucose as fuel. Recent information tells us that coconut oil is an additional fuel for the brain, containing medium chain triglycerides (MCT) which produce ketones.

It is also thought that many of the diseases and disorders to which we are subject are due primarily to inflammation and that the amyloid found in the brain is actually the brain's attempt to deal with inflammation, toxins and infections. In fact, amyloid may be trying to protect the brain!

What activities or learning could you include to stimulate neuroplasticity?

_____

_____

What strategies do you use to outsmart stress?

_____

_____

What strategies do you use to help your memory?

_____

_____

"I've learned that people will forget what you said, people will forget what you did, but people will never forget how you made them feel." — Maya Angelou

Chapter 9

❀

'Mental as Anything'

Chapter 9
'Mental as Anything'

> "Love is not love which alters when it alteration finds,
> Or bends with the remover to remove:
> O, no! It is an ever-fixed mark,
> That looks on tempests and is never shaken."
> — Shakespeare

In 2016 I had the opportunity to present at the National Laughter Wellness Conference in Melbourne, which was organised by the CEO of Laughter Yoga Australia, Merv Neal. I planned to discuss mental health issues, particularly my own experiences of PTSD and how Laughter Yoga really lifted the mood at seminars I had attended called 'Invisible Wounds'. Merv wanted a catchy title so 'Mental as Anything' came to mind.

Mental as Anything is an iconic Australian rock band which initially came together in 1976. Over the years, the band has had intermittent breaks, but is still going strong. They have had numerous hits in Australia and overseas and are extremely well-known and loved. So this title seemed appropriate for this chapter!

Mental health

What do we mean by mental health? According to the World Health Organisation, mental health is "a state of wellbeing in which every individual realises his or her own potential, can cope with the normal

stresses of life, can work productively and fruitfully, and is able to make a contribution to her or his community."

In other words, it is a state of wellbeing in which we are happy with who we are, with how our life is progressing, and we feel connected and have a sense of belonging. Of course, we have already discussed the importance of positive emotions such as love, gratitude, kindness, compassion, optimism, joy, and let's not forget, pleasure, awe and wonder, which contribute to sustaining positive relationships.

When we are experiencing negative or uncomfortable emotions, our wellbeing and mental health is challenged. Severe stress causing anxiety, depression, post-traumatic stress and a sense of powerlessness can have a significant effect on our relationships, ability to work productively and our sense of self. This tends to come under the umbrella of mental illness, which unfortunately still holds a stigma for many people. But reacting to stress is part of the human condition, as well as grief and loss. We need to be more understanding of people whose mental health is challenged by life events. They also need to realise that help is available and seek support long before they are not coping or spiralling down into a place from where they lose hope. Help is always available, but you have to ask for it.

For some people, a type of depression occurs during the winter months. This condition is known as Seasonal Affective Disorder (SAD) and it is important to reduce the risk of this winter depression. It is recommended to remain active, eat a healthy diet and to maintain social connections and avoid isolation.

The more open discussion and education which occurs about mental health and mental illness, the more people will learn to recognise that they need help. Or maybe someone close to them or in the workplace would benefit from support.

Resources for mental health

There are many organisations which focus on improving mental health, reducing the risk of suicide, and providing support for people at risk in the community. We have Lifeline, which people who are distressed can call for support. Beyond Blue is a major organisation in Australia which provides education and support about mental health, particularly depression, which is becoming a significant cause of poor health.

We have 'R U OK? Day' in September and World Mental Health Day during Mental Health Week in October in Western Australia. Services for mental health are very much on the agenda here and there is a recognised need for more community-based services.

There is now a focus on recovery, peer support and education. Lived experience of mental illness often enriches the perspective, resilience and compassion of the individual. Post-traumatic growth is a recognised phenomenon. Many high profile people have shared their experiences of depression, anxiety and bi-polar disorder. This helps to normalise and de-stigmatise these aspects of the human condition.

It is said that one in five Australians will experience a mental health issue in any one year, so it is becoming more important to be open in discussing these matters and the many ways in which people's needs can be met.

Act-Belong-Commit

Act-Belong-Commit is a comprehensive health promotion campaign that encourages individuals to take action to protect and promote their own mental wellbeing, and encourages organisations that provide mentally healthy activities to promote participation in those activities. It was developed through research at Curtin University, Western Australia. It was initially developed for adults but now has components for children.

The A-B-C guidelines for positive mental health provide a simple approach that we can adopt to become more mentally healthy:

Act   Keep mentally, physically, socially and spiritually active. Take a walk, say g'day, read a book, do a crossword, dance, play cards, stop for a chat.

Belong   Join a book club, take a cooking class, be more involved in groups you are already a member of, go along to community events.

Commit   Take up a cause, help a neighbour, learn something new, take on a challenge, volunteer.

Being active, having a sense of belonging and having a purpose in life all contribute to happiness and good mental health. LaughWA Inc. has been accepted as an active partner with A-B-C as our values and goals for improving mental health are in alignment. You will also recognise that many of these recommended activities are congruent with previously mentioned approaches to wellbeing.

Post-Traumatic Stress Disorder (PTSD)

Many people work in occupations that place them at risk of experiencing traumatic and challenging events. These include first responders such as police, firemen and women, paramedics, as well as doctors and nurses. Also, in our wide brown land, many communities are subjected to extreme events such as droughts, floods, cyclones and bushfires. These can provide terrifying and life-threatening events which have a very significant effect on those involved. People involved in serious motor vehicle or train accidents are vulnerable too. Any serious threat to life, which is experienced or witnessed, can lead to PTSD.

PTSD is now a well-known consequence for military personnel. However, this diagnosis was not fully recognised until 1980, although the negative effects of war service were recognised following all the previous wars. Many of the people who served in the armed forces and survived their war service had serious problems with their physical and mental health. The Vietnam veterans are a prime example of the consequences of war service and they have only been receiving the services they need in relatively recent years. There is currently ongoing concern about young soldiers who do not adapt well to civilian life following their stint in the army, which is demonstrated by a significant incidence of suicide. All of this impacts considerably on partners and families.

Two strong, determined and remarkable women whose partners were Vietnam veterans decided to do something about this approximately 13 years ago. Kerryn McDonald and Sam Cross formed an organisation called Partners of Veterans WA Inc. in order to provide support for other partners and their families. They have done this through educational and social events, newsletters and one-to-one support. Over the years, they realised that so many more people beyond the military are at risk of PTSD because of traumatic life events.

Initially, their seminar '*Invisible Wounds*' was targeted at the military and their families. However, in recent years, they have promoted the seminar more widely to include first responders (as mentioned above), as well as anyone in the community who may have experienced trauma. Many people in this situation may not be truly aware that they are experiencing PTSD and that help is available. As an example, a major catastrophic bushfire destroyed a small town in the south-west of Western Australia in January 2016. One wonders how much intervention has been provided to the residents who survived this traumatic incident, and whether they continue to experience the symptoms of PTSD.

So what is PTSD?

Not everyone who experiences a traumatic event goes on to develop PTSD. The information that I am about to share with you is based on a publication from the Australian Centre for Post-traumatic Mental Health.

Certain risk factors include exposure to trauma earlier in life, multiple exposures to traumatic events, absence of social support following trauma and the presence of other major life stressors. Signs and symptoms include having unwanted and recurring memories and vivid nightmares. These are known as 'flashbacks' and can produce an intense emotional response. Hypervigilance, or being overly alert, may lead to being constantly on guard, leading to sleeping difficulties, irritability, difficulty concentrating and becoming easily startled.

People avoid reminders of the event, deliberately avoiding thoughts, feelings, activities, people or places associated with the traumatic event. There may be emotional numbness with loss of interest in day-to-day activities, feeling flat and cut off and detached from friends and family. This can lead to social isolation which is a major risk factor for depression. If these symptoms occur for a month or more and lead to significant distress and impact on the quality of relationships, work and day-to-day life, PTSD may be diagnosed.

Chronic stress of this kind is associated with a wide range of physical symptoms as well. It is common for people to self-medicate with alcohol or drugs when struggling with physical and emotional pain. Intervention requires a holistic approach to address the physical status and mental health of the individual, as the mind and body really are one united system that cannot be neatly divided for the purposes of physical and psychological treatments.

Families of veterans can cope with the support of good community connections, strong relationships within the extended family and with a balanced family life that includes many enjoyable activities. However,

for some, there are serious consequences. Partners of veterans have higher rates of depression, anxiety disorders, sleep disorders and acute stress reactions than partners of non-veterans. In fact, they may be diagnosed with secondary PTSD and if they have also served in the military, primary PTSD!

In civilian life, those who have been exposed to trauma may react in exactly the same way as explained above, but may not be aware of the significance of their symptoms.

Many aspects of PTSD can be treated effectively. Cognitive-Behavioural Therapy (CBT) is recommended for managing depression and anxiety, panic disorder and social anxiety. Expert evaluation and intervention is required and may be needed over a long time. Various therapies include Eye-Movement Desensitisation and Reprocessing (EMDR), exposure therapy, as well as EFT and TRE. Intense therapeutic programs are available for those requiring treatment so that they can improve the quality of their relationships and their own wellbeing, and regain competence and normality in their life.

As mentioned elsewhere, post-traumatic growth can be an outcome for those who achieve a degree of recovery and their experiences can support others.

My Story

I have already alluded to my diagnosis of PTSD and a major car accident where I was in the wrong place at the wrong time! I was given this diagnosis in 2011/2012 by a specialist in stress and trauma. In 2010 I had spent a year on a 'medical mystery tour' following some investigations in hospital which resulted in adverse events, two emergency calls and 19 days in hospital. Unfortunately, my symptoms were ignored as the doctor providing my care considered there was nothing wrong with me. I sought a second opinion and after several specialist consultations, I received four diagnoses!

I had several sleep disorders, was pre-diabetic and finally was diagnosed with a rare neurological condition, as well as PTSD. These conditions were inextricably linked. In previous years, in fact, going back decades, I had experienced episodes of paralysis triggered by severe physical and emotional stress and distress. These episodes resulted in a major stress reaction which was interpreted as mental illness, and the neurologist informed me that people with this particular neurological disorder often had their symptoms misdiagnosed. Low potassium levels are integral to these episodes of paralysis, actually called 'attacks'.

Many years ago, because of challenging life events, I experienced depression, serious enough to be hospitalised. On two occasions I also experienced anxiety and panic attacks which again resulted in hospitalisation. I decided that I did not want to repeat those experiences, which prompted my commitment to outsmarting stress!

In December 2014, I again required some investigations and as a precaution, met beforehand with both the doctors concerned, in an effort to prevent any untoward events. Episodes of paralysis are often preceded by weakness and physical sensations which warn me that they may occur.

When I am paralysed, I am still conscious and fully aware of my surroundings, but I am unable to respond. When I am unresponsive, staff may trigger an emergency call. If I continue to be unresponsive, a painful stimuli is used to obtain a response. There are quite a variety of these stimuli! A chest rub of increasing intensity on the sternum is the most common, pressure on the base of the thumbnail is another, as well as a pen pushed against the great toenail and twisting a finger to the point of wondering whether it would break! As I continued to have frequent episodes, I placed a sign on my chest which said, "KEEP OFF"!!!

Because of additional medical problems, I spent nearly seven weeks in three hospitals, so it was a great relief to go home and take care of

myself. Over the years, I have had numerous ambulance rides and several hospital admissions and emergency calls. Currently I am experiencing my personal best when it comes to staying out of hospital. I have learnt to manage and avoid the triggers, reduce my reactions to stress, nurture my health and wellbeing, and spend as much time as I need recovering my energy.

I consider myself to be very fortunate to have overcome my history. Writing this book is reminding me of the many ways I still need to care for myself with awareness and compassion.

You can also learn to outsmart stress and preserve the health of your body and brain, your mental health and wellbeing! We will explore further aspects of this in future chapters.

What insights have you gained from this chapter?

_____

_____

Who could you turn to if you have a problem?

_____

_____

What resources could you access to improve your mental health?

_____

_____

> "If we really want to love, we must learn to forgive."
> — Mother Teresa

Chapter 10

❀

Make the Most of Moving

Chapter 10
Make the Most of Moving

> *"I exercise every morning without fail.*
> *Up down, up down, then the other eyelid." — Phyllis Diller*

As has been already stated, exercise is a fundamental requisite for health. For some people, the word exercise does not have a very positive response! I believe that movement and physical activity encompass many motivating and enjoyable ways to obtain these benefits. What is really important to remember is that recent research has definitely shown that sitting for long periods is very bad for our health, and many of us do a lot of that!

Working at a computer, doing long distance driving and spending hours watching television equates to a very sedentary lifestyle. People working in offices are recommended to take frequent stretch breaks, alternate between a seated and standing desk, and use the stairs rather than the lift. They could have walking meetings, stand while on the phone and have face to face conversations rather than communicating by email with their colleagues. A lunchtime walk or Laughter Yoga session can help revitalise staff for the afternoon. If convenient, using public transport or riding a bicycle to get to work is preferable to driving.

It has been said that if an exercise pill could be created, and we all took it, we would all be very healthy indeed. So what forms of physical activity do you enjoy? Bear in mind that much movement is incidental, meaning your intention is to achieve something else but you may need to walk to achieve this, i.e. shopping, housework, gardening, walking

the dog and playing with your kids.

What I think of as formal exercise includes specific activities to develop strength, co-ordination, flexibility, stamina and balance, which may include equipment. Resistance training has significant benefits as well as High Intensity Interval Training (HIIT). However, planned exercise can include individual and team sports, gym classes, many kinds of dance, T'ai Chi, yoga, pilates, water sports, multiple kinds of football and ball games, martial arts and numerous adrenalin-charged activities! There are many kinds of bowls including ten-pin, petanque, lawn and carpet bowls. And of course, Laughter Yoga is the most fun of all!

The best form of exercise is that which you actually do! To improve your chances of success, try to find an activity that you really enjoy and can possibly share with a friend or family member. Mall walking has become popular as it is conducted in a safe indoor environment and provides social connection as well. Table tennis has been identified as a very suitable sport as it requires multiple skills but is non-contact.

Dance and enjoy every day

Dancing is highly recommended and is considered to be one of the best forms of exercise. The music creates the mood and benefits include self-expression, the social aspects and aerobic exercise. Your brain has to learn and remember the steps and it provides you with endorphins, so it is a great way to socialise, be active, get fit and improve how you feel.

One of the easiest ways to exercise daily is to put on some jazzy music and express yourself through dance. There are so many dance choices and styles available – circle dancing, belly dancing, line dancing, ballroom dancing, Latin American, swing, and Zumba which you can share with others. However, on your own, you can warm up for the first five minutes, start to dance with your FEET only, then your KNEES, HIPS, SHOULDERS, ELBOWS, HANDS and then with your whole

self for up to twenty minutes, depending on your level of fitness. Use all the dance moves that you know!

If you are dancing with others, especially children, take turns to choose which part of the body you dance with next. Try 'Follow the Leader' or dance with a partner or in a circle to add variety to the dance. This whole routine can take up to thirty minutes, more fun than just walking. Gently stretch for five minutes as you cool down.

If you have not exercised recently, check with your doctor first, and work up gradually within your capabilities. Effective physical activity leaves you puffing, but still able to hold a conversation. Another alternative is to dance vigorously briefly, and then pause for a rest before dancing again. Just pace yourself.

The Feldenkrais Method (FM)

In his book, '*The Brain's Way of Healing*', Dr Norman Doidge devotes two chapters to the Feldenkrais Method and its founder, Dr Moshe Feldenkrais (1904-1984). Dr Feldenkrais was a physicist who completed his Ph.D. at the Sorbonne and he had worked in the laboratory of Nobel Prize Winners, Frederic and Irene Joliot-Curie. During his time in France, Dr Feldenkrais developed a serious knee problem. He was offered surgery, which he declined because it had only a 50% chance of improving the knee. Dr Feldenkrais proceeded to study anatomy, kinesiology and physiology. He combined these with his knowledge of mechanics, physics, electrical engineering and martial arts. The movement to his knee was restored and this marked the start of a lifelong investigation into human function, development and learning.

Dr Feldenkrais subsequently wrote several books, taught his method internationally and he directed the Feldenkrais Institute in Tel Aviv until his death. Dr Feldenkrais believed in the concept of neuroplasticity long before it was validated by the scientific community. He based his method

on the fact that new experiences and information could be integrated in the brain through exploring gentle and non-habitual movements with focussed awareness. There are two aspects to the method – Awareness Through Movement (ATM) and Functional Integration (FI).

ATM

In an ATM lesson, students are verbally guided through gentle exploratory movements in a variety of positions, particularly lying supine to start with, which reduces the influence of gravity. The body is scanned initially to notice how it is lying on the floor, whether it is symmetrical, and which parts of the body are in contact with the floor. A number of often seemingly unrelated movements are repeated and refined with minimal force or effort, usually on one side of the body only. After exploring these movements on the other side of the body, they are eventually combined into an easy and elegant functional movement. There are thousands of lessons which explore every aspect of human movement, often starting with the developmental sequences which we experienced in childhood. Dr Feldenkrais believed that the human body is a cybernetic system in which the whole body is involved in any efficient movement.

FI

In Functional Integration, the student lies on a low plinth and the practitioner uses touch to gently move the student to make them aware of the connections and differences in movement patterns. We often have habitual postures and movement patterns due to life stress, injury and muscle tension and the practitioner shows the student alternate ways to organise movement and posture which is easier and more efficient.

The Feldenkrais Method is widely relevant to enhance human functioning. Dr Feldenkrais used movement as the medium but said that what he really wanted was flexible minds as well as flexible bodies.

The broad spectrum of people who can benefit from the method includes those with movement dysfunction or difficulty at one end of the scale. At the other end, athletes, performers, musicians and actors can all benefit by increasing their awareness to improve performance and reduce the risk of injury. The Feldenkrais Method has been part of the curriculum at the WA Academy of Performing Arts for many years and possibly contributes to the excellent reputation of its graduates.

I was introduced to the Feldenkrais Method by Dr Frank Wildman with other physiotherapists in Australia in 1986. I started my training with Dr Wildman in the Melbourne 1 Training in 1988 and graduated from the Brisbane 1 Training in 1993. Feldenkrais is not a therapy, but is a model of somatic learning which can significantly improve function. At the time, I was working with children and adults with disabilities and movement dysfunction and the Feldenkrais method gave me a learning paradigm to assist them to improve movement function.

To help a small child with Down Syndrome, a lesson is planned on the basis of play, which motivates the child to progress through the developmental sequences necessary to achieve independent walking. These activities can be taught to the parents so that daily play reinforces the learning.

Dr Wildman has published videos and books which recommend the Feldenkrais Method for older people, to help them maintain their youthful mobility and activity. Recommended lessons include improving balance and functional activities such as getting down to the floor and up again, as well as getting out of bed and standing up from a chair. These lessons would also benefit anyone whose mobility has been limited by a stroke, Parkinson's Disease or any other limiting or painful condition.

Your posture

It is wise to be aware of your posture whenever you are seated. The position of your spine, which is elongated above your pelvis, depends on

the position of the pelvis. If your pelvis is rolled backwards then your lumbar spine flattens and you are inclined to poke your head forward, which is not a good functional posture. If you roll your pelvis forward so that you can feel your 'sit bones', your spine will erect itself above your pelvis with all the curves within their normal relationships and your head balanced on your neck. If you are sitting for long periods, i.e. at a computer, having support in your lumbar region is important. However, as we have previously said, changing your posture, standing, stretching and deep breathing will give you a break from prolonged sitting. Some Feldenkrais lessons will assist you to be more aware of your habitual posture and the possibility of a more efficient position so that you can choose between them! We don't lose our old habits, but we can learn new ones with increased awareness.

Your spine has been designed to be flexible and to bear weight. Any time you do lift a weight, particularly from the floor, organise yourself to do so without compromising the safety of your spine. Assess the weight, divide it if necessary and do not lift and twist at the same time. For a very heavy article, ask for assistance and in some circumstances, mechanical assistance is required. For instance, in the health system, hoists are used by staff to transfer patients as it is not considered safe to give manual assistance.

Another story

In a second major car accident, my seatbelt saved my life, but caused a fractured sternum and multiple rib fractures. Needless to say, my posture and movement were significantly restricted! I benefited from several FI lessons which helped me to regain an upright posture (I was leaning to the left and flexed forward slightly). The gentleness and subtlety of the lessons allowed me to re-learn better movement and postural patterns. I regained full mobility of my ribcage without any further consequences. On another occasion, my balance had deteriorated, and again, Feldenkrais lessons helped me to improve my balance. With this

method, the student takes responsibility for their own learning and each lesson creates a state of mindfulness which fully engages the student.

Considerable research has been carried out to evaluate the Feldenkrais method and is available online at www.feldenkrais.org.au

Information can be found at the Australian Feldenkrais Guild and there is a division of this organisation in each state. Practitioners are certified and they offer ATM classes or individual one to one functional integration lessons. Feldenkrais Discovery Days and public workshops are available for people interested in finding out more about, and experiencing the Feldenkrais Method. Trainings are regularly accredited and conducted in Australia and internationally. The International Feldenkrais Federation oversees the research, training standards and development of the Feldenkrais Method.

Up and down from the floor

Specific exercise may be necessary to provide all the requirements that we need to remain truly fit and healthy. We need to develop muscle strength, flexibility, coordination, balance, fitness, bone density and the movement skills to deal with everyday life circumstances. As people age, they are at risk of muscle atrophy and weakness, decreased balance and flexibility, and often have difficulty getting up from the floor if they happen to fall over. Falls prevention is a major concern for our ageing population, which I will deal with in a future chapter.

A Brazilian idea

In Brazil they have evolved a system of assessment to determine a person's ability to get down to the floor and up again safely. The number of supports that the person requires to perform this task correlates with

their potential longevity. The top score is 10, but for every support the score is reduced by 0.5.

So to illustrate this – I am able to sit on the floor by placing one hand on the floor and swivelling down until I am seated on the floor – score minus 0.5. However, to stand up again, I need to place one hand on the floor, swivel my knees onto the floor then push up on one hand and one foot – score minus 2.0. So my total is minus 2.5. This means that my actual score is 7.5. The healthiest range is 8-10, so this is what we should strive for!

(Note to self: Remember to practice getting down to the floor and up again and improve my score!)

It has been recommended that people practice getting down to the floor and back up again five times a day to maintain this skill, which requires strength, flexibility and balance. In many countries, it is part of life to sit on the floor for meals and activities, so this skill is maintained but, in the Western world, our constant use of chairs has reduced this ability!

If you have not sat on the floor for a while, I suggest you try this activity with someone else present in case you have difficulty getting down and up again!

For an older, frailer person, the safest way to get up from the floor is to turn onto all fours and find some stable furniture for support in order to stand up. This needs practice too! Anyone who has experienced a fall which has resulted in injury should have their balance assessed by a physiotherapist. Remedial exercise and education on falls prevention should be provided. People with dementia are at greater risk of falls and it is recommended that they receive falls prevention education at the time of diagnosis.

Movement benefits

It may be pretty obvious by now how important regular movement and physical activity is to our health and wellbeing.

- Exercise of moderate intensity is recommended for thirty minutes a day, or on most days of the week. Walking is probably the most accessible form of exercise and 10,000 steps a day should be the goal. A pedometer or fit-band will do the counting for you and provide motivation to keep heading towards your goal. Even three 10 minute activities can be beneficial.

- Exercise will help you maintain a healthy bodyweight and keep blood sugar and cholesterol levels in the normal range.

- Exercise has a similar effect to antidepressant medication in helping to manage depression and is often recommended as the first intervention. Mood enhancing endorphins are also produced which reward the person who exercises!

- Exercise stimulates blood flow to the brain which receives more oxygen and glucose, and gives existing brain cells a better chance of survival. Studies indicate that regular exercise increases the production of new cells in the hippocampus which is important for learning and memory.

- Strength or resistance training increases muscle endurance, flexibility and improved balance and bone density.

- Do not overlook exercising your pelvic floor. Women who have had children or have reached menopause are at risk of muscle weakness, so if you have a 'wee problem' it is best to see a physiotherapist who specialises in women's health for an assessment and education to ensure your pelvic floor muscles

are contracting properly. You can do your pelvic floor exercises when the ads come on TV, while you are waiting in a queue or at a red light when you are driving!

- Men who have treatment for prostate cancer are at risk of side effects which affect continence and sexual function. It is wise to see a specialist physiotherapist prior to treatment to learn the most effective way of strengthening the pelvic floor so that future management is easier. Recent research at Curtin University demonstrates the importance of exercise for men recovering from prostate cancer.

Many years ago, very sadly, I lost two cousins to prostate cancer, one at 48, and four years later, his older brother at 60. By the time they were both diagnosed, the disease had advanced and treatment was initiated. They both dealt with the diagnosis in very different ways. Steve, my younger cousin, kept the diagnosis to himself, only his boss at work knew. He took long service leave and would meet his mates at the pub after work after having had his radiotherapy treatment! They had no idea! I once asked him, had he noticed that he peed a lot? He said yes but thought it was due to the beer. Is there a lesson in this? Steve also said that he did not share the diagnosis because he didn't want other people to treat him differently.

On the other hand, John let it be known far and wide about his prostate cancer and treatment in order to warn other men about the need for early detection. John had every possible form of treatment and made the most of the four years that he survived. So, as you can see, prostate cancer is not just a disease of older men!

There are so many benefits from physical activity that we all need to find ways to invest our time and energy for our health and wellbeing.

What physical activities do you already enjoy?

_____

_____

What else could you do to increase activity time and decrease time spent sitting?

_____

_____

What is your score getting down to the floor and up again?

_____

_____

"I'm pushing 60 and that's enough exercise for me!"
— Mark Twain

Chapter 11

❀

Sleep Well for Wellbeing

Chapter 11
Sleep Well for Wellbeing

> *"Though sleep is called our best friend, it is a friend who often keeps us waiting!"* — Jules Verne

It is said that we spend a third of our life asleep! This theoretically adds up to 8 hours of sleep a night. But how many of us actually go to sleep easily, sleep without interruption and wake refreshed and energised? There are many barriers to a good night's sleep.

Insomnia has many different aspects:

- Difficulty falling asleep, known as delayed sleep onset.

- Interrupted sleep with frequent waking.

- Waking in the early morning and being unable to get back to sleep.

- Poor quality sleep, resulting in reduced functioning the following day.

Many of us are at risk of sleep deprivation:

- Parents of new babies who require regular feeds 24/7.

- People who work on rosters or night shift.

- Those experiencing stress, anxiety, depression, acute or chronic pain.

- Needing frequent visits to the toilet.

- Having a snoring partner.

- Experiencing sleep apnoea.

- Hearing external noise such as noisy neighbours or a dog barking!

- Teenagers who use social media late at night.

Naturally, a lack of sleep causes fatigue and it is suggested that the effect on driving after being awake for 20 hours is comparable to a blood alcohol level of 0.05. Sleep is needed for regeneration and repair of the body, and although we are not conscious, our brain continues to regulate all our bodily functions.

In order to sleep optimally, we need to organise ourselves and our environment to induce sleep, which is called sleep hygiene.

Sleep hygiene

The following recommendations will help us to successfully fall asleep:

- Aim for 8 hours of sleep.

- Exercise regularly, but not late in the day.

- Avoid caffeine in the afternoon after 2pm.

- Alcohol may relax you, but reduces sleep quality.

- Switch off screens, i.e. T.V. and computer at least half an hour before going to bed.

- Have a warm bath or shower to relax you.

- Go to bed and wake at the same time every day to establish a pattern.

- Avoid sleeping tablets in the long-term as they are addictive.

- Get some sunshine early in the day to stimulate melatonin production and Vitamin D.

- Make sure your bedroom is dark, quiet and cool – use a sleep mask or earplugs if necessary.

- Avoid electronic devices and T.V. in the bedroom – sleep and romance only!

- Have a suitable mattress and pillow.

- Peaceful music may help, as well as chamomile tea and lavender.

- Use relaxation or meditation techniques.

I have had plenty of experience of sleep deprivation! I have delayed sleep onset, probably related to PTSD, as well as early morning waking and frequent interrupted sleep when I wake up, roll over and hope to go back to sleep! Sometimes I do. I find that in spite of many techniques that I have learnt, my brain often stays awake although I am ready for

sleep! I feel that this is a legacy of previous episodes when my brain was on 'red alert' and hypervigilant when I found myself in challenging circumstances.

However, I would like to share with you the many ways I have tried to tame my sleep!

Breathing

As previously mentioned, slow deep breathing has a calming effect on the nervous system. One technique is to count up to four or ten on each out-breath, but return to one every time that you have a distracting thought. I have already shared with you several other breathing strategies, which you can also try to induce sleep.

My latest variation is to say "calm" on the in-breath "and peaceful" on the out-breath. For variation I may say on the out-breath - "and grateful" or "and joyful" or "and sleepy"! The main goal is to quieten my brain so that sleep can take over. It is really important to not become frustrated and irritated when experiencing insomnia because this will just keep you awake! One recommendation is to read a book until you are sleepy or have a warm drink. You cannot force yourself to sleep – you have to invite sleep by providing the right conditions.

Hypnosis

Hypnosis can be undertaken directly with a qualified therapist, who may also be a psychologist. There are also a range of hypnosis scripts available on CDs, downloadable to your MP3 or via the internet or an app. Many years ago, I found that I became very relaxed when verbally

guided by the therapist but was unable to generalise this skill when I wanted to go to sleep. This may have been because my PTSD had not been adequately treated at that time. More recently, I have listened to several different hypnosis downloads with varying degrees of success. You may find them very effective, so they are worth trying.

EFT and SET

I have already mentioned these techniques and it is quite possible to do SET under the bed clothes. SET is said to calm the nervous system when performed consistently for up to an hour a day, and the process focusses one's attention, thereby distracting the brain from unwanted thoughts. Consistency of using SET regularly is important for success.

Meditation and relaxation

Calming the mind seems to me to be the crucial element required to invite sleep successfully. Sometimes my brain wants to keep replaying my concerns and running action replays of what is troubling me. The breathing techniques already mentioned help to put one into a meditative state and relaxing music can help as well.

A relaxation technique which may be helpful involves imagining releasing tension from all the muscles of the body, starting with the head and progressing down to the toes.

- While lying on your back, relax your face muscles so that your forehead is smooth, your eyes are gently closed, your jaw is relaxed, so that your lips are soft and your teeth are not touching.

- Allow the relaxation to flow to your shoulders and down your arms to your hands, allowing them to become heavy and loose as you release tension in all the muscles.

- Release tension throughout your torso, down through your hips, legs and feet. Feel as though you are sinking into the mattress as you release all the tension throughout your body.

- You can then focus on your favourite breathing technique to calm the body, mind and spirit and, as sleep approaches, choose your favourite sleeping position (preferably on your side) and allow sleep to arrive!

It is probably important to persist with the technique that seems to work best for you so that it becomes more effective with practice.

Sounder Sleep

The Sounder Sleep System was devised by a Feldenkrais practitioner called Michael Krugman who is a lifelong student of traditional methods of self-healing. It is available in a self-help audio program which uses synchronized movements and breathing to relax your body, calm your mind, and lull you into sleep. The system teaches slow, gentle minimoves, synchronized with breathing which have a calming effect on the mind and body. Michael trains practitioners across the United States and Europe and has introduced Sounder Sleep to Australia as well. Dr Melissa O'Shea is a qualified Sounder Sleep practitioner based in Perth, Western Australia and she provides classes and individual sleep coaching to help improve sleep difficulties. Practice and persistence are required for success!

TRE

Trauma Release Exercises, as previously described, reduce everyday stress and tension and provide a useful prelude to going to sleep. With practice, it is possible to induce the tremor in the legs after going to bed and allow the neurogenic tremor to develop. A feeling of relaxation

follows as tension is dissipated. One could then follow this with breathing and relaxation.

CBT

Cognitive Behavioural Therapy may be utilised one to one with a therapist or in a group devoted to managing insomnia and enhancing sleep. Strategies may be taught to increase the time spent asleep by going to bed later initially so that fatigue facilitates sleep. Sleep diaries may be recorded beforehand to demonstrate the sleep patterns which need to be improved. Beliefs and attitudes to sleep may need to be reframed to support better sleep, as well as utilising effective sleep hygiene.

Lack of Sleep – Sleep Apnoea

It is quite obvious that lack of sleep causes fatigue and daytime sleepiness. It can also lead to weight gain, increased appetite, raised blood pressure, headaches, irritability, impaired concentration and depressed mood. This situation is further complicated by the presence of sleep apnoea, which results in snoring, with periods of cessation of breathing, causing a drop in oxygen levels. The airway may actually collapse completely which causes a cycle of apnoea followed by sudden waking which happens repeatedly during sleep. As well as the consequences mentioned above, there is an increased risk of heart attack and stroke.

Sleep apnoea eventually triggers a stress response in the brain which causes an intake of air. A spouse or partner may notice this absence of breathing followed by a gasping in-breath. This situation leads to the abovementioned conditions, and needs to be investigated by a sleep physician. Weight control is one of the most effective ways to prevent obstructive sleep apnoea and reduce its impact. Sleeping on the side is also helpful, rather than sleeping on the back when the airway can be occluded by the tongue.

Sleep study

If you have a problem with sleep, you may be advised to have a sleep study, which is usually done in a sleep laboratory. You will be required to stay overnight and a sleep technologist will organise it all. Also known as a polysomnogram, up to twenty different measurements of your sleep and breathing are made. These include measurements of brain activity, eye movement, muscle activity, heart rhythm and breathing. Breathing effort is measured with elasticised bands around the chest and abdomen and blood oxygen levels measured with a probe similar to a clothes peg that is placed on your finger. Leg movements are monitored, as well as snoring and body position, and an infra-red video camera will also keep an eye on you. This monitoring continues overnight as you sleep and the sleep measurements will be analysed and provided to your sleep doctor who will share the results with you.

Continuous Positive Airway Pressure (CPAP) is the most successful treatment which may be suggested. CPAP was invented in Australia by Professor Colin Sullivan from the University of Sydney in 1981. It has now become the treatment of choice throughout the world. CPAP prevents the airway closing by keeping a positive pressure inside it which is applied through a mask attached to the machine, which is small, quiet and reliable. The air can be warmed and humidified and it is important that the mask does not leak. It may take some time to become accustomed to CPAP and it needs to be individually regulated for each person, but some people may notice immediate improvement in their daytime symptoms of tiredness.

Treatment options for sleep apnoea also include a mouth brace, which is fitted over the teeth to gently pull the lower jaw forward to keep the airway open.

If you are concerned about sleep apnoea, you should consult your family doctor who can refer you to a sleep physician. Sleep Disorders Australia has patient support groups throughout Australia.

What concerns do you have about your sleep?

_____

_____

Which sleep hygiene suggestions might be helpful to you?

_____

_____

Do you need some professional help to optimise your sleep?

_____

_____

> *"Laugh and the world laughs with you, snore and you sleep alone." — Anthony Burgess*

Chapter 12

❁

What to Avoid to Achieve Healthy Longevity

Chapter 12
What to Avoid to Achieve Healthy Longevity

> *"Refuse to let an old person move into your body."*
> *— Wayne Dyer*

It is time to take a serious look at the inconveniences, changes, health challenges and losses which may occur as we age. They reduce our chances of enjoying healthy longevity. This information will add to your health literacy and increase your awareness of the importance of making healthy lifestyle choices and motivate you to do so!

It is possible to experience any of the following as we age:

- **Vision and hearing** may become impaired, increasing the risk of isolation and lack of social connection. Patch Adams believes that the worst diseases are fear, loneliness and boredom. This situation may be compounded by apathy, inactivity and depression. Regular assessment and provision of glasses and hearing aids will help people to maintain their social life.

- **Muscle strength**, mobility, balance and stability are likely to decline as we age, increasing the risk of falls, injuries and fractures.

Staying mobile and independent is an important part of healthy ageing. The consequences of a fall can be painful and result in loss of mobility and independence. There are nine key steps promoted by the Injury

Control Council of Western Australia (ICCWA) which help to prevent falls and injuries.

Stay on Your Feet

Step 1:   **Be Active**. Make the most of moving to maintain joint flexibility and muscle strength. This will improve bone density, balance and co-ordination and increase your fitness in order to stay on your feet. Avoid sitting for long periods and stand up and make sure you are balanced before moving off. Beware of inactivity and gravity!

Step 2:   **Manage your Medicines**. All medicines have side effects, some of which can increase the risk of falling. They include drowsiness, dizziness, light headedness, unsteadiness, blurred or double vision and difficulty thinking clearly. Check all your medications with your GP or pharmacist.

Step 3:   **Manage your Health**. Most long-term health conditions can be managed but may increase the risk of falling. Other causes of falls include muscle or joint stiffness, poor vision, reduced concentration, chronic pain and lack of energy. Be mindful as you walk!

Step 4:   **Improve your Balance**. Be active and be aware of factors influencing your balance. Get your balance assessed by a physiotherapist if you have a fall causing injury and be pro-active to prevent further falls! Many exercise and activity groups include balance activities.

Step 5:   **Walk Tall**. Weak leg muscles can lead to shuffling and changes in walking patterns, which can contribute to tripping and make it harder to balance. Use walking aids appropriately and allow plenty of time to go to the toilet.

Step 6: __Foot Care and Safe Footwear__. Take care of your feet and wear correctly fitting shoes with broad heels, which fit well and have good contact with the ground for maximum stability. See your GP or podiatrist if you have foot pain or foot problems, which can alter your gait.

Step 7: __Regularly Check your Eyesight__. Any changes in your vision can contribute to a fall. It is important to see an eye professional regularly so that changes in your eyesight can be detected and managed appropriately. Be careful with new glasses which may alter your perception of the environment, particularly steps and stairs.

Step 8: __Eat Well for Life__. Poor nutrition, skipping a meal or not eating enough at mealtimes can cause dizziness, weakness, light headedness and reduced concentration, all of which can lead to a fall. Choose a nutritious diet and remember that we need to eat more protein for our muscles as we get older.

Step 9: __Identify, Remove and Report Hazards__. Common hazards that contribute to falls at home include slippery floors, clutter or unsecured electrical cords, loose mats or rugs, and even pets. Outside the home, uneven paths, poor lighting and slippery surfaces are a hazard. Observe your environment carefully and walk mindfully to reduce the risk of falls.

BE AWARE OF ALL OF THESE FACTORS
AND STAY ON YOUR FEET!

Let's continue with our ageing concerns!

- **Chronic diseases** such as diabetes, arthritis, cardiovascular disease and stroke may be part of ageing for some people.

However, many conditions are influenced by poor lifestyle choices earlier in life, including cancer. Smoking is a good example. The choices we make now will influence the quality of our health and life in future years. It is never too late to start really caring for your body, mind and spirit! It will be a good investment in your healthy longevity.

Lifestyle and functional medicine is an approach to assessing the causes of diseases, rather than just treating the symptoms. This means looking at nutrition, physical activity, sleep, social connection and the presence of inflammation, deficiencies, toxins and infections. These can all be actively treated to reduce the symptoms of chronic disease. An example would be diabetes or pre-diabetes. With proper nutrition, physical activity and weight loss, blood glucose levels can be stabilised and the need for medications reduced.

Ideally, you need to have a therapeutic partnership with your doctor or any other health professional with good communication and collaboration, which is open and honest so that you can achieve your health goals.

- **Chronic pain** from past injuries, arthritis, osteoporosis and the consequences of surgery may limit people's activities and significantly reduce their independence and the quality of their life. There is, of course, a significant range of pain relieving medications but these need to be taken with care, being mindful of side effects. Some medications can irritate the stomach lining while others affect liver function. Opioids may be needed in the short term for pain relief, but their effectiveness can diminish over time and there is an increasing incidence of accidental overdoses. There is much concern regarding older people having multiple medications with the resulting interactions and side effects taking their toll. Pain management clinics offer multidisciplinary and holistic approaches to managing chronic pain, but require a referral from your GP.

- **Mild Cognitive Impairment (MCI) and dementia** are more likely to occur the older we become. We have already discussed this in Chapter 8, so maybe it would be worth your while to read that chapter again! The consequences of these conditions result in memory loss, personality changes, declining executive function and a gradual loss of independence. The majority of people with dementia continue to live at home with family carers and sometimes need additional support services to maintain the involvement and quality of life of all concerned.

Carers need to be able to care for themselves as a priority so that they maintain their own health and wellbeing. By making all the right healthy lifestyle choices and accepting assistance when it is needed, carers will have a better chance to maintain their caring role and not succumb to illness, resentment and burnout.

If you are a carer, you may be interested in a recently published book by Carolyn Cranwell called *'Navigating Alzheimer's'*. Carolyn cared for her husband for 18 years following his diagnosis of early onset dementia. Carolyn's thought provoking and entertaining style of writing guides the reader gently through sensitive and confronting topics. Her first-hand knowledge and expertise will provide confidence to those wanting to help but feeling uncertain how to approach the person with Alzheimer's, the carer or the family. At the end of each chapter, Carolyn provides 'take-aways' based on her experiences to assist carers in their role. Highly recommended!

Much work is being done to educate health care workers, as well as the community at large, about dementia. It is hoped to reduce the stigma of dementia and encourage better integration of older people into community activities, as this population is expected to increase significantly in the future. There is also a population of people with early onset dementia who require compassionate services.

Prescription for Life is an essential tool for anybody supporting those living with Younger Onset Dementia (YOD). *Prescription for Life* is a free online learning resource funded by the Lovell Foundation, and developed by Edith Cowan University in Western Australia, in partnership with Australian care providers Mercy Health and Bethanie.

Prescription for Life is built around a wellbeing model comprised of seven learning modules: Connectedness, Identity, Security, Autonomy, Meaning, Growth, and Joy. It can be downloaded for free at www.lovellfoundation.com.au

Alzheimer's Australia WA provides education, resources, support groups and respite to assist people living with dementia and their carers. Carers Australia WA also provides multiple supports to carers of all ages to assist in their caring role.

- **Residential care** may be necessary for the individual when chronic conditions or dementia are more advanced. This is a difficult decision which the family may have to make for their safety and ongoing care. This often occurs as a result of a crisis and it is highly recommended that families investigate and plan for suitable options long before they are necessary. However, some of the consequences of dementia may include apathy, agitation and depression, all of which can be managed in an effective and compassionate way.

- **Frailty** can be part of ageing as well and may contribute to decreasing autonomy and independence, resulting in a move to residential care. This loss of the familiar home life can be distressing, but there are now many programs to assist people to remain in their own home. A philosophy of re-ablement commits to encouraging the individual to use as many skills and perform as many tasks as possible so that they can regain a level of independence and self-confidence. Maintaining social connections and enjoyable group activities reduces isolation as well. It sometimes happens that the frail person's health and vitality improves with the additional care.

- **Losses** may be involved with ageing, many of which we have already mentioned. The death of a spouse, a relative or a close friend is a significant loss which seems to occur more frequently as we get older. The remaining spouse may have to learn many new skills in order to live independently and safely. It may be necessary to downsize, although in some states house-sharing with a younger person (possibly an overseas student studying English) provides company and support. These well-organised arrangements benefit both parties, with the student providing a specified number of hours of support in return for accommodation, and improving their English. This arrangement allows the older person to continue to enjoy living in their own home and also delays admission to residential care.

- **Hospitalisation** is sometimes a health hazard for much older people who are already frail, have several chronic disorders and possibly some degree of dementia. If they are confused and in an unfamiliar environment, they are at risk of falls and fractures in hospital, as well as infections and skin trauma. So staying healthy and avoiding falls is a big priority! The confusion is called delirium and may be caused by an infection, or by anaesthesia and surgery. Delirium can be treated by reversing the cause. Some older people may also be depressed and it is a significant challenge for medical staff to correctly diagnose and treat delirium, depression and dementia.

- **Effective palliative care** is an important priority towards the end of life, and provides effective symptom control and emotional and spiritual support for the patient and their family. There is a growing need for palliative care to be available, not only for cancer patients, but also for those with chronic diseases or degenerative disorders. People with dementia also require palliative care, whether they are at home, in hospital or in an aged care facility.

- **Care options** may be appropriate for the individual for their optimal safety and wellbeing and they may need to be admitted into a Residential Aged Care Facility (RACF). It is impossible for a family carer to provide 24 hour care to someone who needs it. The person concerned has to adapt to a new environment, different carers and a whole change of lifestyle which conforms with the organisation of the facility.

  There are several different philosophies of person-centred care which prioritise the individual's needs for privacy, choice, engagement, wellbeing and quality of life. The aim is to make life as similar to home-life as possible, involving people in everyday activities. In the past, staff tended to do everything for the residents, i.e. serve cups of tea and meals. Over time, the residents will be encouraged to serve their own tea and meals, laying the tables and helping with other domestic tasks which are a normal part of life. This allows for more interaction with the staff and other residents and builds self-confidence. Outings, pets, gardens and arts-based programs contribute to a better quality lifestyle.

  There are many different programs and activities to involve people experiencing dementia. With memory loss, they are confined to living in the present and need to feel safe, valued, comfortable and engaged in enjoyable interactions and activities.

- **Environments** are especially designed to ensure that people can move around freely using good lighting and simple signs to guide them. In the Netherlands, an entire village with shops and a theatre has been created so that the residents can easily enjoy the facilities. The village is also available to the public and allows for a very unrestricted lifestyle for the residents. Group homes are another way of providing a home-like atmosphere for a group of people with dementia who are also involved in everyday domestic and recreational activities together.

It becomes quite obvious, doesn't it, that for some people there is a certain trajectory towards old age, which may diminish their health and abilities. However, many older people remain very competent and independent and the number of centenarians around the world continues to grow.

What concerns do you have about your health?

_____

_____

Which lifestyle choices would help to improve your health?

_____

_____

What help do you need to achieve your health goals?

_____

_____

"Thinking happy thoughts literally creates positive chemical changes in the brain which stimulates both positive, physical and psychological benefits." — Deepak Chopra

Chapter 13

❁

Top Tips from the Centenarians of the Blue Zones

TIPS!

Chapter 13
Top Tips from the Centenarians of the Blue Zones

> "An archaeologist is the best husband
> any woman can have; the older she gets, the more
> interested he is in her." — Agatha Christie

What are the Blue Zones, you may ask? Much research has been carried out on unique populations of centenarians in several areas around the globe. Scientists were interested in discovering the factors that contributed to their longevity and one of them circled these regions with a blue marker pen! Hence the Blue Zones, which include several remote mountain areas and islands where the traditional culture and lifestyle has persisted.

These Blue Zones include the islands of Sardinia in Italy, Okinawa in Japan, Costa Rica and mountain regions in the Russian Caucasus, the high mountains of the Hunza region in the Himalayas and the Ecuadorian Andes. A high proportion of centenarians have also been found on the Greek island of Ikaria and at Loma Linda in the USA. On a trip to Mauritius a few years ago, I came upon a book called 'Centenarians of the Republic of Mauritius' by Karrim Esshack RMN, PSW. He discovered a significant number of centenarians during his social work career and his book about them is very illuminating! However, I don't think anyone has put a blue circle around Mauritius yet!

Dan Buettner, in his book, 'The Blue Zones', outlined the healthy habits, nutritious diets and the cultural and family values that each longevity

society upholds. He found that particular lifestyle habits were found in common in each of these Blue Zones societies, such as (and I quote):

- Emphasis on strong family values.

- Strong community values.

- Exclusively plant-based diets (little to no animal products).

- Antioxidant and anti-ageing plants are plentiful.

- Daily benefits of physical exercise.

- Everyone knows how to deal with stress.

- All the elders and centenarians still do useful work.

- A sense of purpose in life.

- Spirituality is part of life.

- A complete absence of smoking and obesity.

- Everyone knows the benefits of a positive attitude.

However, in each location in the Blue Zones, there are specific aspects of their lifestyle and diet which can guide us.

Sardinia, Italy

Here they eat a plant-based diet with occasional lean meat and their diet consists of beans, wholegrain breads, vegetables and olive oils. They have a glass or two of red wine daily and the men often gather in the

street daily to have a good laugh with their friends, resulting in lower levels of stress and reduced risk of cardiovascular disease. They have strong family values, particularly for their elders, and put family first. Walking is their usual form of exercise.

Okinawa, Japan

The Okinawans also rely on a plant-based diet which includes stir-fried vegetables, tofu, sweet potatoes and bitter melon. They are all involved in gardening, which provides daily exercise and daily produce includes the medicinal plants turmeric and ginger. Okinawans are also active walkers and, as they enjoy their meals seated on the floor, they strengthen their lower body muscles sitting down and getting up. Social circles are important for working and security. Females aged over 70 are the longest-lived population in the world.

Costa Rica

Here they have a family focus, generally living with their families, and have a strong sense of purpose, maintaining relationships with friends and neighbours. They eat lightly and work hard throughout their lives, which they enjoy. They keep up with traditions. They have the world's lowest rates of middle-age mortality and the second highest concentration of male centenarians.

Ikaria, Greece

The Ikarians eat a Mediterranean diet including fruit, vegetables, wholegrains, red wine and olive oil. They drink goat's milk and herbal teas and enjoy a mid-afternoon nap, which helps to reduce stress. They walk and garden in mountainous terrain which contributes to their fitness, and social connection is very important. As members of the Greek

Orthodox Church, they fast on a regular basis. Research demonstrates that the only proven way to slow the ageing process is to reduce calories by 30%. This Aegean Island has one of the world's lowest rates of middle-aged mortality and dementia.

Loma Linda, California

These Seventh Day Adventists live ten years longer than their North American counterparts. They maintain a healthy body mass index by keeping active and eating sparingly, including lots of legumes, and they drink plenty of water, but do not drink alcohol. They are involved in voluntary work to help others and take a break on the Sabbath to be with family and friends, nature and God. This time together strengthens social networks and relieves stress.

Mauritius

The islands of Mauritius and Rodrigues, which are of volcanic origin, are ideal for growing vegetables which are the common foods, together with fruits and fish. Red meat is only used on festive and religious occasions. Rice and lentils form part of the diet as well but dietary preferences were reported by the centenarians as seafood and vegetables. The clear lagoons also provide an abundance of kelp which has many health benefits and is also an important part of the diet of the people of Okinawa. The centenarians adopt a positive attitude by keeping good relationships, adapting to change and coping well with diversity. They had worked very long hours to make ends meet, walking more than six miles daily to go to work on the sugarcane fields. They maintain a positive attitude, making the best of what they have, recognising and accepting emotions and staying active and keeping family and social contacts.

My Story

A few years ago, I fulfilled a long-held dream of travelling to Mauritius. One of my patients, years ago, was a lovely woman from there, Helene, who had had a stroke at quite an early age. Over time we became friends and I was able to practice my French with her. Helene was able eventually to travel with her son to Mauritius on a couple of occasions, which she originally had thought impossible.

My trip to Mauritius was on a spectacular cruise liner with my friend, Ann, who was an intrepid and frequent traveller. I was delighted to discover that she was happy to share the trip with me. As you can imagine, life onboard was luxurious, with wonderful food, service and entertainment. Early on day three of the nine day trip, I missed a step and fell heavily on a very hard marble floor, severely twisting my right foot and left knee. I waited until the next day to see the doctor, by which time there was considerable swelling. He asked me why I had waited to see him and I replied that I was an optimist!! My foot and knee were strapped up and I spent the remainder of the fourteen day holiday limping and popping Panadol! I wasn't able to join in the dancing, but I did enjoy the French classes. I used the lifts instead of the stairs and found much to enjoy in spite of my discomfort. It is true that pain is inevitable, but suffering is optional!

Once we reached Mauritius, we spent several days sightseeing with a couple also from Perth. Three of us sat in the back seat of a taxi and I have to admit that getting in and out of the car was very painful, as my knee didn't want to bend! However, the location was beautiful, the food was delicious, the service friendly and the demonstration of the local Sega dancing made me want to join in! The girls wore very long skirts which they undulated as they vigorously gyrated their hips – they must have been very fit! I treated myself with a couple of massage sessions and really had a wonderful time!

The highlight of the trip was a visit to a safari park where we were able to visit some lions and actually pat them! I had always wanted to have this opportunity, as a children's book called '*Lionel Lion Laughs at Last!*' is one of the resources in '*The Nurturing Kids Kit*'.

Blue Zone's Lifestyle

Dan Buettner and his team at National Geographic, having studied the world's longest-lived people, came up with recommendations to help the average person increase their life expectancy by 10-12 years by adopting a Blue Zone's lifestyle.

1. **Move Naturally**

   Centenarians live in environments that regularly motivate them to move as they walk often and grow gardens but don't use modern conveniences for house and yard work.

   (We tend to be very sedentary and need to look for opportunities daily to walk, climb stairs, use public transport rather than drive and choose physical activities that we enjoy to promote our fitness and health.)

2. **Purpose**

   Having a sense of purpose is worth up to seven years of extra life expectancy. The Okinawans call it 'Ikigai' and the Nicoyans call it 'Plan de vida', meaning 'why I wake up in the morning.'

   (We all need a reason to get out of bed in the morning, someone or something to love, something to do and something to hope for.)

3. **Down Shift**

   Stress is experienced even by people in the Blue Zones. Every major age-related disease is associated with stress. Centenarians have daily routines to reduce stress. Okinawans take a few moments each day to remember their ancestors, Adventists pray, Ikarians take a nap and Sardinians do happy hour!

   (I have already shared multiple strategies to outsmart stress! Take your pick!)

4. **80% Rule**

   People in the Blue Zones eat their smallest meal in the late afternoon or early evening and then nothing more the rest of the day. The Okinawans say "Hara hachi bu" before meals to remind them to stop eating when their stomachs are 80% full.

   (Judging when you are 80% full probably takes a bit of practice but is worth the effort!)

5. **Plant Slant**

   Legumes including beans and lentils are a significant part of most centenarian diets and on average meat is eaten five times per month – portions about the size of a deck of cards.

   (There is growing concern about eating red meat, and its effects on the individual and on the planet. Diversify your menu with eggs, fish, vegetables, legumes, fruit, nuts and seeds.)

6. **Wine @ 5**

   Except for Adventists, people in all Blue Zones drink alcohol moderately and regularly. Moderate drinkers outlive non-drinkers. It is preferable to drink one to two glasses per day with food and/or with friends. And no, you can't save up all week and have 14 drinks on Saturday!

   (Red wine is a preferred beverage as it contains an antioxidant called Resveratrol which has health benefits. Drinking a glass

of water in between alcoholic drinks is recommended, as well as eating food with your beverage.)

7. **Belong**

The majority of centenarians interviewed belong to a faith-based community. Research shows that attending faith-based services, whatever the denomination, will add years to your life expectancy.

(Even if you do not belong to a faith-based community, you can belong to many other organisations and groups which give meaning and connection to your life. I belong to a worldwide Laughter Yoga community and really treasure my 'tribe' of Laughter Yoga friends.)

8. **Loved Ones First**

Successful centenarians in the Blue Zones put their families first. Ageing parents and grandparents are kept in the home or nearby. They commit to a life partner and invest in their children with time and love, who will eventually care for them.

(In Australia, different generations do not always live together or nearby, although this is the practice of many migrant families who have enriched our life and culture here.)

9. **Right Tribe**

The world's longest-lived people chose - or were born into - social circles that supported healthy behaviours. Okinawans created 'moais' – groups of five friends that committed to each other for life. Research shows that smoking, obesity, happiness, and even loneliness are contagious.

(Research has demonstrated that you tend to share the characteristics of the five closest people in your life! So finding friends with the same values and attributes will support you to achieve your goals around health and life.)

All this information can inspire us to look at our own lifestyles and investigate how we can improve our own health and wellbeing and contribute to our own healthy longevity.

It is worth noting that Okinawans who have migrated to the USA and adopted the American lifestyle and eating habits eventually acquire the same lifestyle diseases. Also, younger Okinawans have been influenced by the importation of American style fast food and sugar-laden drinks. By adopting these Western foods and forsaking the traditional nutrition of their culture, they too are succumbing to obesity and chronic disease.

What food choices could you make to improve your longevity?

_____

_____

How could you improve your social connections and sense of belonging?

_____

_____

What strategies could you use to reduce your stress levels?

_____

_____

"Age does not protect you from love. But love, to some extent, protects you from age." — Jeanne Moreau

Chapter 14

❀

Summary –
Now it's Up to You!

Chapter 14
Summary – Now it's Up to You!

> "Life is short. Break the rules. Forgive quickly.
> Kiss slowly. Love truly, laugh uncontrollably and never regret
> ANYTHING that makes you smile." – Mark Twain

Dear Reader, there is much diverse information in the preceding chapters, some in more detail than others. My intention was to share what I have learnt over many years, decades even, which I hope you might find useful. Perhaps you are already familiar with some of this information. But on the other hand, your curiosity may have been aroused and you might like to find out more about particular aspects of health and wellbeing, which you can add to your repertoire.

What is important to remember is that your body/mind/spirit form an integrated whole. Centuries ago, Descartes declared that the body and the mind were separate, but we now know better! What occurs in your body influences your mind and vice versa, and all this influences your very essence, your spirit. To give you some examples, if you happen to feel depressed, this will be expressed in a posture which is slumped and protective. Our body language reflects how we are feeling and our emotions. In fact, we embody our emotions, which means that if we decide to take on an upright confident posture, this will influence how we feel.

The placebo effect works if we believe that a 'sugar pill' has healing powers, which demonstrates the connection between the body and the

mind. Even anticipating an enjoyable or amusing event can have a positive change on our physiology.

This is why Laughter Yoga, in which we create playfulness and positive emotions including joy, is so successful at contributing to a feeling of wellbeing. We may start off feeling quite flat but our intentional laughter can become genuine and we get that wonderful dose of happy hormones – Dopamine, Oxytocin, Serotonin and Endorphins. Here the actions of the body improve our mood, as well as giving us a dose of aerobic exercise.

We have looked fairly thoroughly at many strategies to reduce stress and enhance wellbeing. I suggest that you find time to revisit these and choose some. You can add these strategies to your life on a regular basis, to create new habits and outsmart stress. We are all well aware of the negative consequences of stress and we need to regularly monitor our status in order to identify our early signs of stress, so that we can intervene efficiently with a healthy option. We achieve much because of the challenges in our lives but it is important to schedule recovery time – small nurture breaks during the day, good quality sleep and holidays!

Our nutrition is a key element which contributes to our health. As you know, there is a vast amount of information available on this topic via all the print and digital media. If you wish to obtain further information, make sure you access reputable websites and well-qualified people with suitable credentials and credibility. Over the years, much nutritional information, which was initially seen as appropriate, has been reversed. Many foods thought to be unhealthy are now considered appropriate. Healthy fats are an example, also coffee, eggs, red wine and dark chocolate!

Many people choose to be vegetarian or vegan, some for health reasons, and others out of concern for the environment and the welfare of animals. Whatever your beliefs, increasing your plant intake can only provide benefits for you and your health.

The healthy choice list is just a reminder of the many factors we need to consider to optimise our health. It seems to me that as we get older, taking care of our health and wellbeing could become a full-time occupation! Building in healthy habits every day makes it easier to achieve our health goals. Sometimes it helps to create a daily chart of all the healthy activities you need to include in your life – of course, you need to remember to read it!

(Note to self: That's a great idea which I must remember to do!)

There is currently so much information about dementia and Alzheimer's in the media and on television, that it is a constant reminder to preserve our cognitive abilities. It is important to create events that are worth remembering so that you build up a collection of positive memories. Over and over again, exercise is recommended as the primary activity to incorporate into our daily lives to preserve our brains. Exercise increases the size of the hippocampus which holds our memories. Do you have enough movement and physical activity in your life? Have you considered how to make the most of moving?

(Note to self: When this book is finished, I would like to get back to table tennis for the social benefits and the many skills required to keep the ball hitting the table!)

Music is a powerful means of stimulating memories, as well as altering our mood and helping us to feel calm and relaxed. Music may make us feel sad, but can also make us want to sing and dance, which are

such life-enhancing activities. Singing in a choir has been demonstrated to have significant benefits, not only on the respiratory system, but the social aspects, belonging to a group with meaning and purpose, and sharing the joy of music.

Although I have mentioned yoga and T'ai chi, which have demonstrated benefits, I prefer the Feldenkrais Method which I feel will help me to preserve my functional mobility and balance as I get older. I would like at some time in the future to participate in T'ai chi as it is a graceful moving meditation, requiring mindfulness and having a positive benefit on muscle strength and balance.

(Note to self: Haven't you been promising yourself to attend some tango lessons?)

Do you sleep well or is night time a continuing challenge? There is plenty of information and help available should you need it. Sleep is another important contributor to our health and wellbeing so make sure you are getting optimal quality and quantity of sleep.

Love Laughter and Longevity

There are some key points which I would like to reiterate to help you on your journey to healthy longevity.

- Take responsibility for your own health and wellbeing. This is a lifelong challenge and requires you to outsmart stress and develop healthy lifestyle habits.

- Be your own best friend and nurture your body, mind and spirit based on self-awareness, self-respect, self-appreciation and self-compassion.

- Give and receive love! Remember Vitamin L? Make the most of Vitamin F and Vitamin P so that you feel loved and appreciated by those closest to you, and can reciprocate so that you have a sense of belonging and validation.

- Live in the present moment as often as possible. In doing this, you are not focussing on past negative events or future concerns. Remember that the brain cannot tell the difference between the actual experience and what you remember of it. It will therefore bring up the same emotions as the actual event. Remember to strengthen the positive pathways in your brain by **'Taking in the Good'**.

- Improve your ability to recover from stress and develop resilience. Post-traumatic growth is now recognised as a consequence of becoming stronger, more resilient and compassionate following recovery from challenging circumstances.

- According to Dr Patch Adams, it is important to avoid fear, loneliness and boredom! Social connectedness is essential for our emotional health and volunteering is a very appropriate way to connect with other people, contribute to their wellbeing and, at the same time, fulfil the essentials for your own happiness.

- Ageing is said to be biochemical rusting – which is really about the effect of inflammation, toxins and free radicals on your health. A diet rich in vitamins, minerals, fibre and antioxidants will contribute to healthy ageing, although the right genes do help!

- Optimal nutrition requires healthy food choices and eating less to contribute to longevity. An adequate intake of water for

hydration is essential and reducing the intake of chemicals of all kinds is an important priority. Extra vitamin and mineral supplements may be helpful if you have a deficiency. I find that coconut water is useful for hydration due to the electrolytes it contains. It was actually used as IV fluid during World War II in the Pacific because of its similarity to plasma!

- Physical activity every day has multiple benefits, allowing for adequate recovery time. You will keep your body in good shape as you age, maintaining muscle strength, flexibility, balance and stamina. You can exercise your brain with new challenges, activities and learning which will maintain and develop new neurons and pathways, adding to your cognitive reserve. Exercise your sense of humour as well so it is there when you need it. If you lose your sense of humour due to significant stress, ask for support to deal with the problem causing it. A 'humorectomy' is an early warning sign which you cannot afford to ignore!

For all of the above, **Use it or Lose it**!

- 'Stay on your feet' – as we have already described, there are multiple factors to be aware of in order to prevent falls, injuries and fractures. So take the time to check these out and stay safe on your feet.

- Laughter IS the Best Medicine! Check out your Laughter Prescription and make sure you invite more laughter into your life. You can do this either in your social interactions or at work, by focussing on the positive and amusing aspects of life. You can initiate your own Laughter Therapy by accessing more comedy and humour via the media, or of course, finding a Laughter Club and participating in Laughter Yoga. It's up to you!

- We are all on this journey together, so maybe it would be helpful if we share this relevant information. We can support each other to develop the healthy habits that we need, to stay healthier for longer. Good health means we have the energy and the physical ability to get the most out of life. So plan and act now for a healthy and enjoyable future!

What can you add to your life to improve your chances of healthy longevity?

_____

_____

What information would you like to follow up in the resources section?

_____

_____

How are you going to reward yourself for good behaviour?

_____

_____

"Become the director, producer, choreographer of your own story." — Deepak Chopra

Final Words

Final Words

Dear Reader, you seem to have arrived safely at the end of this book. My intention was to share with you multiple ideas, strategies, techniques and activities which might contribute to your health and wellbeing, and help you to achieve healthy longevity. Some topics I have explored in more depth, others just superficially, so in no way is this a definitive version!

However, you may find that much of this information confirms what you already know, but perhaps about which you have not yet taken action. On the other hand, there may be much that is new to you, which will inspire you, arouse your curiosity and convince you to find out more!

In the resources section, you will find a bibliography, references, relevant websites and organisations which can provide you with further information. I challenge you to keep pursuing your own optimal health and wellbeing. In future years you will be able to look back! You will feel really pleased with yourself that you made the right decisions and took the actions which now contribute to your good health and quality of life.

As for myself, revisiting all this information has made me aware of areas to which I have not paid enough attention. I will be setting up my own set of goals and support systems to assist me to practice what I preach! I hope that you will do the same!

Finally, I hope that this book will make a difference in your life and I would like to close by sharing words of a well-known Loving Kindness Meditation.

May you be safe.

May you be well.

May you be happy.

May you be free from pain.

May you live your life with ease.

May your life be filled with love and laughter.

We who laugh … last!

Love Laughter and Peace

Janni

Author Profile

Author, Speaker, Wellbeing Educator and Laughter Yoga Leader, Teacher and Ambassador

Janni Goss is a conference speaker, wellbeing educator and author specialising in sustaining wellbeing and taking responsibility for one's health throughout life. Janni is a qualified physiotherapist and Feldenkrais practitioner, and a former lecturer at the School of Physiotherapy in Western Australia. She was initially trained in 2000 by Dr Madan Kataria, Founder of the Laughter Yoga Movement, and subsequently in 2005 and 2008.

Janni is the Advisor for Ageing and Disability for the National Council of Women Western Australia and promotes healthy longevity. She is currently the President of LaughWA Inc. which provides Laughter Yoga trainings, and supports the establishment of Laughter Clubs in Western Australia.

Janni is the author of the book *'Love Laughter and Longevity – The Art and Science of Wellbeing'*.

Janni's travels have taken her to Canada, Malaysia, Singapore and Europe. In Geneva, Janni worked as an au pair to improve her French, worked as a physiotherapist in England, and visited Oslo, Norway to pursue her interest in childhood asthma. She enjoyed the Edinburgh Festival and skiing in Austria and Switzerland. Janni presented at an

International Health Education Conference in Ottawa, Canada and more recently spent time on the island of Mauritius, where she discovered that there is a population of centenarians – of great interest.

Janni has presented at numerous international, national and state conferences, as well as at corporate events and professional development seminars, health and education seminars. She is invited to present at women's, carers and seniors' organisations, retreats, fundraisers, expos and AGM's.

Janni has a particular interest in the wellbeing of children and created JelliTime™ to help children learn relaxation and self-regulation skills. Movement, fun, laughter and relaxation are integral to JelliTime and it utilises the elements of Laughter Yoga as part of the engaging activities. Janni has produced a Nurturing Kids Kit to promote children's wellbeing, which has been featured on the Today Tonight program on Channel 7 in Perth, Western Australia.

In 2006 Janni was the recipient of a Laughter Ambassador Award from Dr Kataria at the first Australian Laughter Conference and in 2012 she was the convenor of the first West Coast Laughter Conference in Perth. Sebastien Gendry, CEO of Laughter Yoga America, was the keynote speaker. Dr Kataria gave his presentation at the Conference via Skype.

As a result of her life experiences, Janni is passionate about outsmarting stress and specialises in sharing multiple strategies to improve health and wellbeing. She has taught stress-reduction strategies to thousands of adults to help them take care of their health and sustain their wellbeing.

Her presentations include her Laughter Prescription and introducing participants to the wide range of benefits that Laughter and Laughter Yoga provide. Janni has been affectionately known as The Laughter

Lady since 2001 and is widely known for her presentations which are inspiring, interactive, informative and fun. Janni was invited to have a profile in the book 'Motivational Speakers Australia' which was published in 2015.

Janni is a member of the Australian Physiotherapy Association, Australian Feldenkrais Guild, Council on the Ageing (COTA), National Seniors Association Australia, Australian Association of Gerontology, National Council of Women WA, Early Childhood Australia and OMEP (International Pre-school Education Organisation).

Janni lives in Perth, Western Australia but frequently visits Melbourne to spend time with her son, Simon, his wife, Miyo, and her new grandson, Ethan.

Recommended
Resources

❁

Recommended Resources

Are you looking for an experienced speaker at your next Conference, Team Development Program or Function? Janni will tailor her inspirational presentation to suit the challenges and aspirations of your organisation.

Presentation Topics

- **Is Laughter the Best Medicine?** - An interactive workshop on the health benefits of Laughter and Laughter Yoga. Is Laughter the Best Medicine - try a dose to find out!

- **Laughter as Therapy** - Discover how to utilise the benefits of Laughter and Laughter Yoga in the Health and Ageing sector for staff, clients and patients.

- **Love Laughter and Longevity** - Explore how to outsmart stress and improve the quality of your life.   Get the most out of your longevity by making healthier lifestyle choices. Laughter and optimism may add years to your life!

- **Outsmart Stress for Workplace Wellbeing** - Outsmart workplace stress with multiple strategies including healthy lifestyle choices, emotional intelligence, resilience, positive attitudes and creative solutions, and of course Laughter! Work Smarter, Not Harder!

- **The Art and Science of Wellbeing** - Wellbeing Theory from Positive Psychology promotes positive emotions and relationships.   Explore daily strategies for wellbeing, starting with gratitude and including healthy choices, and the benefits of Laughter.

- **Wellbeing Matters** - Shares the best strategies to help carers prioritise their own wellbeing, so that they can successfully continue in their caring role.

- **Laughter Yoga Training** - Learn how to facilitate Laughter Yoga in your workplace with colleagues and clients, community groups or start up your own Laughter Club. Invite more Laughter into your life and share the gift of Laughter with others.

- **Nurturing Kids - JelliTime™** - Explore the finer points of using the Nurturing Kids Kit to Play, Learn, Laugh and Relax with the children in your life (from 3-8 years old). The Kit has all the resources you need to learn how to play JelliTime™ with children and would be useful for parents, grandparents, childcare staff, paediatric therapists and early childhood teachers.

    The Kit is available at www.jannigoss.com

For further details visit these websites:

www.jannigoss.com

www.MotivationalSpeakersAustralia.com/Janni-Goss

There are so many diverse topics in this book that I thought it would be easier to provide publications, as well as websites, which you can explore for free information, videos, workshops and products. You can easily find any information by 'Googling' the author's name, book title or relevant key words.

Please pursue the topics that interest you as lifelong learning is one of the keys to longevity!

Other Resources

Chapter 1   Outsmart Stress for Healthy Longevity

*   Dr Rick Hanson - Positive Neuroplasticity '*Hardwiring Happiness*' (2013) - www.rickhanson.net

Chapter 2   Is Laughter the Best Medicine?

*   Patricia Cameron-Hill & Dr Shayne Yates '*Stress, Humour and Health*' - www.chy.com.au

*   Dr Patch Adams '*Gesundheit*' (1993) - www.patchadams.org

*   Dr Madan Kataria & Madhuri Kataria '*Laugh for No Reason*' (1999) - www.laughteryoga.org

*   Norman Cousins '*Anatomy of an Illness*' (1979) - www.archive.org/details/AnatomyOfAnIllness

*   Dr Lee Berk Ph.D. '*Mind, Body, Spirit: Exploring the Mind, Body, Spirit Connection through Research on Mirthful Laughter. Spirituality, Health, and Wholeness, An Introductory Guide for Health Care Professionals*'. Haworth Press, 2004 - www.llu.edu/pages/faculty/directory

*   The Smile Study - *The Sydney Multisite Intervention of LaughterBosses and ElderClowns (SMILE) study: cluster randomised trial of humour therapy in nursing homes* - Journal of the American Medical Directors Association Volume 15, Issue 8, August 2014, Pages 564-569 - www.dementia.unsw.edu.au

*   AATH - USA - Association for Applied and Therapeutic Humor - www.aath.org

*   The Humour Foundation Australia - www.humourfoundation.org.au

- Laughter Yoga Research-South Africa Dr Gita Suraj-Narayan www.ukzn.ac.za/UKZNonline/V3/17/s16.html

- Australia - *Laughter yoga activities for older people living in residential aged care homes: A feasibility study* - Ellis JM[1], Ben-Moshe R[2,3], Teshuva K[4]. www.ncbi.nlm.nih.gov/pubmed/28699684

- Australas J Ageing. Australasian Journal on Ageing Volume 1 No. 1 (2017)

- Prof Paul Bennett - Australia - www.deakin.edu.au

- Paul N Bennett, Trisha Parsons, Ros Ben-Moshe, Merv Neal, Melissa K Weinberg, Karen Gilbert, Cherene Ockerby, Helen Rawson, Corinne Herbu, Alison M Hutchinson, *Intradialytic Laughter Yoga therapy for haemodialysis patients: a pre-post intervention feasibility study,* BMC Complementary and Alternative Medicine, 2015, 15, 1

- Ros Ben-Moshe '*Laughing at cancer*' (2017) - www.laughlife.com.au www.laughingatcancer.com

Chapter 3   The Laughter Prescription

- Good News Network - www.thegoodnewsnetwork.org

- Good News Movement - www.facebook.com/GoodNewsMove

- Dr Madan Kataria - www.laughteryoga.org

- Merv Neal CEO of Laughter Yoga Australia - www.laughteryogaaustralia.org.au

- Sebastien Gendry USA The Laughter Consultants - www.laughterwellness.org

- LaughWA Inc. - www.laughwa.org.au

Chapter 4   The Science of Wellbeing

- Dalai Lama - www.dalailama.com

- California Riverside Campus - www.ucr.edu

- Positive Psychology - Dr Martin Seligman - *'Flourish'* (2011) www.authentichappiness.sas.upenn.edu

- Professor Marc Cohen (RMIT) - www.profmarccohen.com

- SEWB - *Aboriginal and Torres Strait Islander Community Health Info* - www.healthinfonet.ecu.edu.au

- Yorgum Aboriginal Corporation, Health Services - www.yorgum.org.au

- Dr Nic Marks - www.nicmarks.org

Chapter 5   More Strategies to Outsmart Stress

- Breathing 4-7-8 - Dr Andrew Weil - www.drweil.com / www.youtube.com/watch?v=gz4G31LGyog

- Mindfulness - Jon Kabat-Zinn - www.mindfulnesscds.com

- Thich Nhat Hanh - www.thichnhathanhfoundation.org

- Dr Ian Gawler - www.iangawler.com

- David Michie – *'The Dalai Lama's Cat'*, (2012) *'The Art of Purring'* (2013), *'The Power of Meow'* (2015), *'Why Mindfulness is Better than Chocolate'* (2014) - www.davidmichie.com

- EFT & SET - Steve Wells - www.eftdownunder.com

- Nick Ortner - www.thetappingsolution.com

- TRE - Dr David Berceli - www.traumaprevention.com

- Richmond Heath - www.treaustralia.com.au

- Hidden Wounds - www.partnersofveteranswa.org.au

- Workplace Wellbeing - Spencer Johnson '*Who Moved My Cheese?*' (1998)

- Laughter Yoga - www.laughwa.org.au

Chapter 6   The Art of Wellbeing - Simple Pleasures

- Hygge - www.visitdenmark.com/hygge

Chapter 7   Love, Respect and Nurture Your Body, Mind and Spirit

- Susan Peirce Thompson Ph.D. '*Bright Line Eating*' (2017) - www.susanpeircethompson.com/bright-line-eating

- Tara C. Mitchell '*Outsmart Sugar*' (2016) - www.outsmartsugarnow.com

Chapter 8   Treasure your Brain

- Dr Norman Doidge '*The Brain That Changes Itself*' (2007) - www.normandoidge.com

- '*The Brain's Way of Healing*' (2015) - www.normandoidge.com

- Dr Jenny Brockis '*Brain Fit!*' (2013) - www.drjennybrockis.com

- Dr Daniel Amen '*Making a Good Brain Great*' (2006) - www.danielamenmd.com

- Dementia - Alzheimer's Australia - www.fightdementia.org.au

- Alzheimer's WA - www.wa.fightdementia.org.au

Chapter 9   'Mental as Anything'

- Life Line - www.lifeline.org.au - *Phone 131 114*
- Beyond Blue - www.beyondblue.org.au
- RUOK Day - www.ruok.org.au
- Mental Health Week - www.mentalhealth.wa.gov.au/events/mentalhealthweek.aspx
- World Mental Health Day 10th October - www.1010.org.au
- Act Belong Commit - www.actbelongcommit.org.au
- PTSD - www.defence.gov.au / www.beyondblue.org.au/the-facts/anxiety/types-of-anxiety/ptsd
- PVAWA - www.partnersofveteranswa.org.au

Chapter 10   Make the Most of Moving

- Feldenkrais Method - Dr Moshe Feldenkrais - www.feldenkraismethod.com
- *Australian Feldenkrais Guild Inc.* - www.feldenkrais.org.au
- Dr Frank Wildman - www.feldenkraisinstitute.org/frank-wildman
- David Beard - www.exerciseiq.com.au
- Australian Physiotherapy Association - www.physiotherapy.asn.au

Chapter 11   Sleep Well for Wellbeing

- Sleep Australia - www.sleepoz.org.au / www.sleephealthfoundation.org.au
- Dr Michael Breus Ph.D. - www.thesleepdoctor.com
- Sounder Sleep - Michael Krugman - www.feldenkraisresources.com/Rest-Assured-Self-Healing-for-Insomnia-p/2013-mp3.htm

- Dr Melissa O'Shea Perth, W.A. - Repose Sleep Solutions - www.melissaoshea.com
- Sleep Apnoea - CPAP - www.sleephealthfoundation.org.au

Chapter 12   What to Avoid to Achieve Healthy Longevity

- Falls Prevention - ICCWA - www.iccwa.org.au
- MCI/Dementia - Alzheimer's WA - www.wa.fightdementia.org.au
- Dementia Training Australia - www.dementiatrainingaustralia.com.au
- Dementia Support Australia - www.dementiacentre.com.au
- Eden Alternative - www.edenalt.org
- Prescription for Life - www.dementiatrainingaustralia.com.au/prescription-for-life-supporting-those-living-with-younger-onset-dementia
- Spark of Life - www.dementiafoundation.org.au/introducing-spark-of-life
- Carolyn Cranwell '*Navigating Alzheimer's*' (2016) - www.Navigating-Alzheimers.com

Chapter 13   Top Tips from the Centenarians of the Blue Zones

- Dan Beuttner '*The Blue Zones*' (2008) - www.bluezones.com

Chapter 14   Summary - Now it's up to You!

Additional Resources - Organisations

- National Seniors Australia - www.nationalseniors.com.au

- Council on the Ageing (COTA) - www.cota.org.au

- Carers Australia - www.carersaustralia.com.au

- Carers WA - www.carerswa.asn.au

- Australian Red Cross - Carers Support Services - www.redcross.org.au

- Dr Joseph Mercola (reliable source of health articles) - www.mercola.com

- Dr Mark Hyman (health information) - www.drhyman.com

- WA Association of Mental Health (WAAMH) Peak Organisation for Community-based Mental Health Services - www.waamh.org.au

www.ingramcontent.com/pod-product-compliance
Lightning Source LLC
Chambersburg PA
CBHW071956090426
42740CB00011B/1958